AZALAR PUBLISHING
Suite 114, 2675 W. Hwy. 89A
Sedona, AZ 86336

THE WRITINGS OF THE
MANTIRA

Book 1

by
George Goulding

Azalar Publishing
Sedona, AZ

ISBN 0-9624831-1-7

published 1991
AZALAR PUBLISHING
Suite 114, 2675 W. Hwy. 89A
Sedona, AZ 86336

printed by
Light Technology
Sedona, AZ

dedicated to
GLORYNN ROSS
who knows about liberation

with gratitude to editors:
RON HOGGART
KATHLYN KINGDON
MARGARET PINYAN

art by MARLYS K. POWELL
front cover, **"Moon Tablet"**
back cover, an oil rendition of a Jean Franck bronze,
"Oh, To Be Free!"

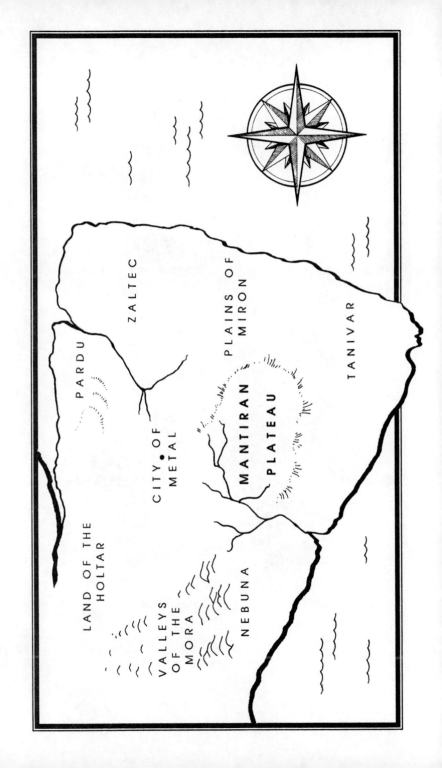

CONTENTS

FOREWORD

These writings are for those of you who once lived in a certain time and area of this planet. Their purpose is to reawaken in you the spiritual properties that were highly developed and much used in that place and period.

Persons not from then and there may find little of interest here, for they probably will not respond to the flavor hidden within the picturizations and the style of wording, a flavor that was part of that general culture.

It is said that these writings have achieved sixty to sixty-five percent success in their attempt to reproduce the images and feelings of that time and place. It is said that even thirty percent is considered fortunate in inspirational transcription.

The vehicle of that era was fire.

INVOCATION

A z a r,

From the icy caves of fear
I watch for You.

From the ancient grove of law
I wave to You.

From the balcony of self
I sing to You.

From the ash heap of desire
I come to You.

And from the threshold of my love
I bow to You.

PROLOGUE

The men of Manti marched into the land of Pardu and met the men from the other lands who were gathered on the third elevation. The groups were formed, and clothing adjusted to the loose tunic, for this was to be the dance to the Sun, to Azon the Sun. (This was in the early days before the rise of the civilization that culminated in the metal city and before the awareness of Azar, the Total God.)

The drums and flutes started, and the men began the movements of the Sun dance, forming circles that swirled and crossed each other. In the heightened light of Azon their awareness quickened, and as they moved they acknowledged each other, showing the feelings that were part of their fullest regard for Him — for Azon is the god of the masculine, of strong and heat-producing movements, and they were sharing their love and respect for Him with each other.

His glorious Sun-love began to appear and spread among them, and they discarded their tunics in a move toward fullest intimacy with Him. When His ecstasy was complete within them they stopped and stood motionless, allowing their entirety to be embraced by Azon, and allowing their bodies to worship in their own way, to project their essences out into His brilliant light, projections brought forth by the deepest feelings of intimate oneness with Him and His holy Being!

Then they moved away, stronger and more sure, full of His joyous light and intimate love. Their arm clasps were genuine, their feelings of brotherhood were strengthened, and their regard for each other was greater than that achieved by agreement on parchment.

They returned to their lands and families full of dignity and grace, with the strength of Azon within them and the glow of His heaven upon them.

THE CITY OF METAL

And so we left the City of Metal: a city of metal machines, metal actions, metal feelings, metal God. We left to find the Natural, to live again with the planet Earth.

Metallic fog covered the metallized land for several days' journey, and we grew discouraged. But Alphon stated that the Natural should be no more than three kilims away, so we continued on. The overcast began lightening, that which Alphon called the sun began showing through, and we were generally excited!

Soon the sky was clear. We were standing on a promontory overlooking valleys and hills, a beautiful rolling vista, and it was *green*! The sun was hot and burning, so Alphon drew us under an overhang, explaining that we must accustom our skins to the rays of the sun in short periods, which we did. We rested, and wondered why man had gotten so far away from all of this, why the call of metal had been so hypnotic.

1

When asked, Alphon said there was a legend telling of men living beneath the surface of the earth, who, due to the proximity of deposits of metal, become metallized, so to speak. They at times send hypnotisms up to the surface men which entrap them, making them also enamored of metal. The men on the surface then imitate the interior men, in time becoming metallized as well. We could not but believe this, considering the way our fellows were becoming, there in the metal city.

Adjusting ourselves, we continued toward a lofty plateau in the distance, a tall, confident plateau. We had many adventures on the way, with strange animals, plants and things. Several of our people were lost due to fallings and drownings. We grieved, then moved on. Arriving at the base of the plateau we found a hidden path which we climbed, tortuously, and with exhaustion reached the top.

It was a paradise! Trees, running streams, and beautiful meadows filled with wild grains, fruit-bearing plants, and vegetables. We explored, shouted, and ran through areas, looking. No other humans were there. They must have been gathered up by the great search of years ago.

We sat together in a wooded glen and Alphon explained that we would have a community, a loose, free, community; that we would mark out parcels of land for development, with people working individually or together. He said we would be happy and productive and that we would be called...the Mantira.

He then told us of Azar, of His being our creator and protector. He explained that for some time all knowledge of Him had been suppressed in the metal city. It was felt that such knowledge would distract people, causing them to want to be independent, thereby interfering with their efficiency; that the knowledge wasn't important anyway and probably not true. Instead they were taught that their origin came about through the desire of physical cells to form groupings; that through this desire the chemical action of the cells brought forth entities whose natural qualities of intelligence and personality were from the cells themselves. As a result of this teaching, cells became deified, with the symbol of a cell grouping used as a worship point.

Alphon then told us the true story of our creation. He related how Azar had caused His angelic workers to invent the human body system and then to form souls from the high essence, placing them within these bodies and creating a place for them — the planet Earth. He explained that we, these souls, live many lives on Earth, between which we are gathered back into the Other Place for rest and instruction. Then returning to Earth we inhabit new bodies, with new problems to work out, new disciplines to be learned, and new happinesses to be accomplished!

He said the reason for our being constructed and placed here was to create companions for the Deity, to furnish workers for His cosmic areas and vessels for His holiness. We were here for these purposes and none other and so should get on with it.

He told us the metal peoples' leaders were rebelling against this holy Plan. He said rebellion *was* allowed, it being known that sooner or later the rebels would return to their senses. Unfortunately, the time of their advancement would have been altered and some character damage done which would require a certain amount of energy to repair. He said that we were a group whose destiny was taking us from the metal setting so that we could grow and strengthen and become ready to pick up the pieces, the nonmetal pieces, when our brothers' insanity was done.

So we started our new existence. Periods each day were set aside for physical activity, for lumbering, farming, and the like; and other periods for the mental, for schoolings and learnings of the laws of this earth and universe. Additional periods were devoted to the spiritual — for the contact, Alphon explained. He said we must again link with Azar, our source. This linkage had been temporarily severed in most of mankind, and we needed to reach out with our center soul (in the middle of the body, as he showed us) and through our eitic energy, grow, as it were, another linkage. This would be done through purposings, through visualizings, through energizings, and, most importantly, through lovings.

He explained that our interest and desire would attract helpers from above. They would come to succor us, to give us vibrations, growing vibrations. These helpers would be invisible to us because of our broken linkage; however, as the contact grew we would again begin to see and hear them, which would enable them to help us more directly.

He told us that after one set of helpers had accomplished their instruction, another group would appear, carrying us on to new learnings. Our linkages would strengthen, being fed by meditational vibrations and by the reaching toward us of loving energies from the Higher Realm. This would continue over a number of lifetimes, in between which we would receive direct instruction in the Other Place. Then, coming back in intimate groups, we would continue our growings here.

In the meanwhile the metal people would be degenerating, their path being one of self-destruction. It is said that those under the surface are followers of one fallen helper who, rebelling against the Way, cast himself out of the Higher Realm. He fell like a falling comet, striking and gouging deeply into this planet; however, being in an eternal body as all higher helpers are, he did not die, but lay stunned within the earth for centuries. Finally coming to himself, he began to plan and work beneath the surface, creating his own creatures, the ones who become metallized, and using them to find ways to oppose *the* Way and ways to create his own, the metal, way.

Alphon said that even the fallen helper will one day change and desire help, and that a highly placed one will then come down to aid him, to gently lift him up again and give him the special love they had known before, when they were the first twins to be created, eons ago.

And so we lived, believed and worked. Some of us are now in a third living here. Records are being kept, with full explanations of purposes and occurrences. We have already found other rebellers from the city, lost and wandering on the plains, and have helped them at lower camps, bringing them to our plateau only after all traces of metal have disappeared from their flesh, particularly from the areas of their lungs.

One of them, an older man who had been an official, told us that the city is now aware of us and is contemplating the building of an aerial device to carry explosives to our land to lay waste our homes, fields, and animals. We have consulted our white-clad guides, the helpers that are presently with us, and have been told that the Other Place knows of this plan (which originated in the mind of the fallen one who is the anti-helper) and that energies are being prepared there to counter this attempt. The device will be turned and allowed to fall on the city itself, effecting much damage and thus fulfilling the prediction of Zelan. This disaster will break up the cohesion of the city, causing its inhabitants to spread out and be drawn back into nature, to ultimately enter our lower camps. The highly placed helper will oversee these happenings, and at some point directly confront his fallen twin, who will then be offered the Grace of Redemption. As to what will happen after that, the veil is drawn. Even our highest contacts know no more than this.

So we are preparing for our part in the occurrence.

Stores of food and healing chemicals are being gathered both here and on the plain below and new techniques for demetallizing are being studied. Direct worship of the Highest is being instilled at all levels. This will bring additional energy. Our goal is to learn to better love our fallen brothers and to help them in their cleansing. To inspire them, in spite of their metal negativity, to raise themselves up to our plateau. Long periods of time will be required, but we are committed, yes, and honored to be given the grace of this undertaking. We will serve the High One with all of our strength and purpose. We will ever continue to be His earth arms and hands, His earth eyes and ears, His earth loves, giving His holy love to His holy children, for His holy purposes.

A-mena.

THE TALISMAN

When the fire was first seen in the evening heavens, we were amazed! As the flame rose higher and higher we felt our love flowing toward the one trying to contact us, so we moved quickly to the stone calling device in the lee of the mountain, and sang.

Our behest was answered. He came to us, his chariot pulled through the sky by two white fire-horses, confidently moving. At our feet he dropped the talisman, the gold-metalled form we still use for the callings in our ceremonies. We believe he came from another age, that in the sky is a transfer point for harmonies to move from time-point to time-point. His face was serene; his hands had been dipped in fire.

Dropping the talisman, he turned sharply and sped off in the direction of Sirius. Later we charted his journey. Its angled configuration forms our forehead symbol to this day.

Within the talisman we found a printing thus stating:

> "This seeing is for those in the far distance. We bring to them these knowings which are to be perceived as the truths of all existent beings.
>
> "Know that all being is one, for all live within each other. What benefits one benefits all. What hurts one hurts all.
>
> "If sickness, or off-vibrating, comes too frequently and pain crowds too closely, then an awareness of destiny and a glimpse of personal purpose is needed, for all beings must Fit.
>
> "Only those not Fitting have sicknesses. The harmony of being in one's place, knowing and doing one's Fitting activity, is guard against such possible off-vibration. All aspects and organs are then in curious alignment with each other, pulsating harmoniously.
>
> "The sense of Fitting, to be activated, needs to ride on a personal respect and love — a respect for the Structure and a love of the Plan, the invisible Plan behind the Structure. "

Then followed an elaboration of these principles, with procedures and explanations carefully given.

We were amazed and a little appalled. Imagine — to love without reservation the invisible, the unknown. To respect, yes, but to *love?* It staggers the imagination! However, the sick were calling to us, sharing their pain with us. We had to try. We had to learn how to Fit.

So we began. First, as was suggested, we constructed a basic story symbology. Working from feeling points we realized that all things within the Structure were Planned and then created by Azar, the Planner-Creator; that within the original Planning we do Fit, as do all the creatures and objects here; that as legitimately Planned beings we need to understand this Fitting, and to fulfill it.

Having come to these realizations, we started the project itself. We began sending forth an awareness of respect for the Structure, followed by deep feelings of love and commitment to the Plan. We had been told that by doing this our inner vibrations would harmonize enough to form a balance upon which the Plan could imprint an instruction of activity, of a Fitting activity that would be our own.

Our tellers of the future, using the milky-white stones, have been declaring that in six orthons of time, based on Eliron's movements, there will be gigantic numbers of souls living on this circling earth shape, the majority of whom will not be Fitting, but will instead be off-vibrating. Sickness will be rampant, with no one knowing why except the few the charioteers will inform, if they stand at a stone calling place such as ours. (I understand there are several more within the lands.)

We applied ourselves daily to this activity and soon things were happening. New feelings began to rise, take form, and *shimmer.* This excited us, causing us to work even harder and to take a further step. Calling in four of our more imaginative and adroit young people, we asked them to devote all their time to the project, becoming test cases, as it were.

After several diams of time they reported back — and oh, such a marvel! — were glowing and filled with the deepest feelings of peace and happiness and were accomplishing brilliant new things! Almar, in constructing a living shape, found himself placing the surfaces in such a way that the interior had much more light and air. Frena discovered a new way of starting sparks for the morning heatings. The disfiguring red marks on Alteen's face and body disappeared after he ate on impulse a certain plant growing in the hills. And Zima, at a mysterious urging from within, placed her hands upon the midsection of our leader during one of his swelling attacks. Heat formed at the point of contact, and within a short time his pain was gone. The four of them were supremely happy and confident in their new activities. They were obviously Fitting!

We discussed all of this at a night meeting and agreed that the printing was right. If one truly harmonizes with the planning mechanism behind the Structure, It, in turn, will indicate what one's Fit pattern is and how to enact it.

The evidence became even more conclusive. Almar designed living spaces that remained above the ground, giving freedom from the small creatures. Frena cast heating devices, quite compact, yet effective. Alteen collected plants, and dispensed their dryings to those with various needs. And Zima healed many with her touchings, even those with the dreaded flesh-wasting sickness.

So we applied this Fitting sequence with even more vigor: first, feelings of deep respect for the Structure, then active love and commitment to Azar's Plan behind it.

The people were divided into small groups, each with a positive leader, and patterns were formulated for those whose imagination was lacking. We worked hard at this. Through long nights and days we applied ourselves with zeal and humility, purposing all for the Plan, not for ourselves.

This was twelve recorded turnings ago, and one can now see the results. Faces are vibrant with eyes fresh and quick, and hands are facile, moving to inspired doings. Our nourishments are diverse and simply prepared. We are poised, confident and joyous.

We have been given more information about the Plan, and are ambitiously moving with it. We have been told that we are here to grow in certain ways, mainly in the way of service to each other and to the Plan; that when we are truly serving, the Great Joy will appear and cause us to at times tremble. (This has already begun in the gatherings!)

We have also been informed, our seers are so honored, that we go on from here; that this is but one step in an endless journey, with each step presenting new challenges and fulfillments; that Azar, the Master Planner, watches over all of our improvings, and His dedicated ones help us from their neighboring places, volunteering to do so as a serving. We have been told that we are here to develop the ability to love, and that the depth and breadth of this development determines the level we go to at the next Stopping, the degree of beauty we step into at that time. We meet many times in many places during our journeyings, which helps the loving of each other. And we recognize that a high ecstasy is intended us. (A few have already experienced glimpses of this and have reported back, radiant and bemused.)

The groupings around the water shores have become aware of our surging forward and are now inquiring, seeking instruction in the new ways. So some of us are going forth as teachers. One young man, in his own way, is particularly adept at this. Our seers have seen that one day on this same circling earth shape he will furnish the earth body for a master teacher (one of the early sons, possibly even the legendary first Son), who will appear and instruct untold numbers of souls through many orthons of time. He will teach in person at first, then later through writings. People will call unto this teacher, "Hosanna!" and he will be the first to be instructed by the great Planner in how to avert and even reverse the Stoppings, and how to embody himself as he so wills.

We are now happy, secure, and loving. We know our future is glorious, and that our destiny marches on. We know that we are and always will be gods, and that one day we will be Co-Planners with Azar; Co-Planners serving Eternity!

THE HOLTAR

We bring you the ways of the Holtar, who ruled the deserts and hills near Mora. Their numbers were legion. Never had such a people been seen. They were strong, secure, and filled with lightning. They walked with large movements, their shoulders supple, their hands filled with grace. Their arrogance, though, was unmistakable. They fell, finally, during a summer storm on the desert. With pennants trampled, they lay everywhere, stunned by the unseen. Bodies twisted, with hands reaching for an anchoring, they fell.

May the gloss of pride be wiped from the brothers in the streets. May the parade of vanity be stopped through the mirror of critical examination. May love for Azar outweigh all belief in personal prestige and may the conqueror's display of captives and animals become a barbarism.

Let us state further that the Holtar were a great and clever people, full of accomplishment and design. They worshipped the hard, straight lines of the body and the pull of the muscles. They felt that man was a master, not a servant as Alphon's people believed. They felt that man could own the emotion of superiority, whereas Alphon's people, the Mantira, knew that man was a vessel to be filled and used by the universe. The Holtar saw man as an instrument to be wielded in the service of dominance. The Mantira saw him as an instrument whose wielding should be dominated by Service.

So the Holtar moved against the Mantira. Their swords were sharp and whistled piercingly. Their instruments of destruction were polished with respect, and their imprecations were practiced and deadly. They did not hope; they knew. They did not ask; they stated. They did not heal; they cut. Forward they marched, with robes swirling, eyes glowing, and voices humming at a fixed pitch of energy.

Alphon and his circle gathered at the tip of the plateau, watching the machine of the Holtar advance across the plain. Alphon's eyes were remarkably bright, considering his age and length of service. He stood in advanced position, a solitary beacon against the sky. The Holtar drew near with a rush of chariots, a neighing of horses and a blaring of trumpets. They regarded Alphon with proud lips and probing eyes. They observed the gold at his wrists, the stones at his neck — all fashioned with love for the beauty of Azar. The Holtar, resplendent and alive in their judgments, dismissed him as of no consequence.

At a specific moment Alphon signaled with his left hand and the elements of Zin came and placed a barrier of darkness before the Holtar.

We weep for you, Children of Holtar. Know you

not that you are already immortal and possessed of the universe? That you have no need to acquire, that all, all is yours? You are puny children, with foolish notions and tiresome ways — thoughtless children to be stopped, to be given no permissions, to be allowed no tramplings, for the earth is fragile. Indeed, the vines are tender and the young trees break easily. You rude souls, you make of destruction a sign of superiority. The stopping of you will probably bring your disintegration, for you equate balance and sanity with conquest. Take away your swords and you fall into chaos.

Let it be known that the Elements of Zin were at one time the recipients of a large gesture from the Mantira. Zin is a position, a location in the time frame adjacent Earth. The linkage point with this frame is at the boundary between Mantira and a neighboring race. A number of direns ago this race became deeply afraid of the linkage point, therefore of the Zin, and summoned with chantings, invisible forces, causing them to be arrayed at the opening of the point, pressing around and upon it, creating a paralysis, a stoppage — corking the opening, as it were. The Zin were then in distress within their time frame, for circulation of magnetic impulses is necessary between the frames. It is like blood in an earth body: stop it moving and the organism dies.

Yes, the Zin were endangered, as were the endangerers also, and a hurting pulsation issued forth and vibrated through to this side. The Mantiran seers, perceiving it, investigated with their milky-white stones and learned the history of the problem. Traveling on universal rays with their physical bodies left behind, they moved through the forces and into the linkage point, where they conversed with the Zin. They explained that the problem with the neighboring race was one of confusion, not of intent, and obtained the Zin's approval of an agreement. Then, visiting the people of the earth race, they reassured them and told them of the the nature of the Zin and of the proposed agreement, achieving acquiescence there also.

And so the siege was ended. The agreement consisted of a pledge by all never to block the linkage point and never to enter the other's area without an invitation. The Zin were grateful to the Mantirans for this and offered their assistance, if ever needed.

Now the Mantira had known for some time that the Holtar were planning to confront them militarily, and had tried in many ways to avert this happening. Hoping to build a bridge of friendship, they had sent peace missions, science committees, artists and performers, and speakers to promote brotherhood and explain Azar. They had sent gifts and had meditated and prayed. They had, in fact, used every form of influence possible, wishing only for the Holtar to grow out of their childish pursuits as the Plan intended. They hoped that the winds of change would lead the Holtar into less destructive paths and would, in fact, normalize them. They always, however, kept as a last resort the possibility of calling on the Zin.

Which is what ultimately happened. After trying all alternatives and seeing them rejected, they summoned the Zin. After checking all factors for rightness, the Zin agreed to help.

The heart of Alphon was heavy but open, seeing the Holtar as young ones being given a correction and being placed again on the right path. Alphon knew well that no one truly dies, that one simply goes elsewhere for awhile and then is back again, correcting old patterns. Better the Holtar fall now, he reasoned, so that their new chance could come sooner.

The Zin, summoned, stated their plan. First, the dark

curtain, to warn. Then, if necessary, the use of reverse matter to negatively polarize their metal weapons and crumble them.

The proud Holtar advanced, feet keeping the complicated battle step. Up to the black curtain they moved, then paused and touched the blackness with their weapons, which became cold and eerie, sending back to their holders imagery both strange and alien. Men of maturity would have reconsidered at this point, but not the Holtar. Since the first contact did not kill them, they abruptly shouldered their way through and continued on.

The Zin now dispersed a cloud of reverse matter, gleaming yellow-green in the sunlight. When it touched the Holtar weapons they crumbled into yellow-green dust, staining the ground. The Holtar faltered and broke ranks. With eyes flashing, the leaders called the men back into order. Shouting that they would now use the method of Salin, they and their men donned black gloves on their right hands, closed ranks, and advanced, making grasping motions and shouting with defiance. (The method of Salin: strangulation with one hand.)

Although the Holtar were still some distance away, Alphon was kept informed by his seers, who observed the black gloving of the troops. He quickly called a conference with the Zin. They discussed the situation and an ultimate decision was made. It was decided to stop the Holtar by stopping the breath of the Holtar themselves.

The Zin carefully prepared the powder and gently wafted it from the plateau toward the black-gloved Holtar. As the undulating purple cloud met the Holtar, there was a chanting from the Zin, a request to the Over-All for care and attention to these souls whose Earth lives were being interrupted. The Holtar fell, and with straining lungs looked at the Mantira with eyes begging compassion. Alphon made the sign of grace, which they dumbly acknowledged.

Then the sheen faded from their faces and their souls left their bodies, to stand quietly apart. The Shining Ones came and led them away, carefully and with regard.

Alphon, whose inner sight could perceive such scenes, later told us of this, of the cloud of Shining Ones gathering in the spirits of the Holtar and putting a white substance on their chests and throats to quickly dissolve the physical memory structure of the suffocation, thereby preventing the necessity for any kind of later reenactment of the incident, reenactment in a later living to purge the storing mind of such a frightening memory. The white salve was effective; the memory content was dissolved.

The spirits of the Holtar were led away to the Other Place, and stillness returned to the desert. The Mantira buried the remains of their foes, then prepared large caravans of supplies to take into the land of the Holtar for the surviving families. The Mantira then began an instructional program, to bring the remaining Holtar to Azar. This instruction was correlated (through the Mantiran seers) with what was going on among the Holtar warriors in the Other Place to ensure that when the former family groupings were reborn together again, they would all have similar beliefs and understandings.

The Mantira also held special meditational knowings for the Holtar daily for many years. Finally, it was fully ascertained that all the Holtar had risen above this incident, which later became known as the day the flowers of death bloomed on the lower plains, and God harvested the Holtar Children, whose numbers were legion.

THE SQUARE

We came early that day, knowing the portents to be correct. We came early, and could tell by the carbonation that the explosions from the firing of the Porgas had been fairly recent. The land was barren, with hardened sludge lying in piles. Yet it still had its holy atmosphere, the atmosphere the Work had brought, which was now a part of the very soil, despite the recent fire-purging.

By breaking up and moving the configurations of melted rock and sand, we cleared the prescribed dimension. Room enough for the Others to "land," as it were, and stand with us — how many of them we would not know until later when Carla, our seer, would look back and describe.

We placed ourselves, ten on each of the four sides. We have found that the square has different properties than the circle has, and is better for the result we were striving for: not healing as such, (the circle is better for that), but direct growth through stimulation of the body's wheels of light. Carla had reported that the wheels in a number of us had become somewhat discolored and were not free and loose, neither revolving nor in a state of readiness to do so.

Danan put us in the proper order, balancing the sexes and the types. Osan would be the progenitor, the focal rod — the seed, so to speak.

We sang and chanted our lovely music of sound and words, music that uplifts the feelings toward our beloved invisible Azar; and at the same time predictably calms the body and orients its mechanisms to the proper countings: the normal heartbeat, intestinal movements, brain vibrations, and glandular flows. This placed us in a condition of near-weightlessness, our feet touching the ground only as a symbol of relationship to it. Soon we would experience levitation, showing us again that our inner essence can be free of dependence upon the Mother, our beloved Mother Earth.

Danan took the curved rod, with its connecting arms of baked glass, and held it at the proper angle to the ground. The energy came and the arms moved to a horizontal position, in line with and powered by the circling vibrations of the planet. (Earth still has its energies, despite the cataclysmic activities of the Children of Darkness.) Suddenly the vibrations moved upward, and we were lifted and placed standing on top of the circling ray-vibrations, some eighteen kilers above the earth! All of this brought about the necessary conditions for the most important activity, the working within the relationship, the personal relationship with Azar. The being-one-with-, the conversing-without-words-with-, the knowing-the-actual-heartbeat-of-, Him — Azar, our Main Love. Many call Azar the Father, but to us He is simply the *Main Love*, the most loved of our many loves!

Thus we were positioned properly: up, without fear,

trusting Him and His forces. Danan said the proper words and little Osan made the proper movements. (These are intuitive, and differ with each Mover. They cannot be passed from one to another.) Osan was particularly lithe and graceful that day, beautifully positioning the limbs of her body (neighbors, she calls them, seeming to give them an intelligent awareness of their own). The link was being formed. We were being put in an harmonic attunement that would allow intimate contact with Him.

Then the vibratory rollings began to build and crescendo. (These are the harbingers.) Our eyes sparkled and we cast upon each other glances of love and trust. We held hands, treasuring each other, letting our souls intermingle. Finally we knew that Azar was with us. (He always is, of course. However, in this happening we achieve the ability to directly apprehend Him, so we speak of it as His coming *to* us, even though we know that He is everpresent.)

His ineffable Grace was now upon us. We saw the White in the center of the square, the divine White. It moved to us and surrounded us. Our primary colors were visible and looked so beautiful, mingling with the White next to our darker skins. (Our skins are dark from relationship with Azon, the Sun, the incarnating vehicle of our previous planetary leader.)

As the White, the symbolic White touched us, we heard Azar within, our Main Love. He spoke to each of us differently. (We tried to compare conversations later, but could not.) He spoke so personally, it was as though a higher, finer part of ourselves were talking. He was so open to us, instructing us lovingly in secrets beyond measuring, in intimacies going far beyond the pale range of the average human closeness. The union was complete, the knowings and feelings identical, the harmony deep and profound. There was no thought of separation or difference; we were *one*, in the sweetest most loving way. Naturally, our beings responded to this, for they were being given a chance to be normal, to be truly healthy, to glow!

And glow they did, and sing! The organs, particularly those near the solar plexus, pulsed and purred with pleasure. The wheels turned gracefully, and from them darted the most beautiful colors. The forehead eye opened with its trusting love and saw the Others, the glorious Others there with us, our beloved brethren, giving to us of their love and energy. We raised our arms together, all of us, and in an immense and awesome voice spoke the Celestial Word!

The air trembled and surrounding nature gathered close, wanting to share the experience. So we purposefully sent the energy of gratitude and love to our brother objects, the material substances near us. They responded with brilliant colors and flowing energy patterns. The very soil beneath us was living, moving, and the rocks around us were mysteries of color. The plants and trees opened their leaves and lifted their arms, straining skyward. A hawk flying overhead swooped down and settled on Danan's head, with talons of velvet and eyes of widest ecstasy. The energies (what a mild word for what we are speaking of) now began a rhythmic swirling, bending, and pulling. We gave, moving and swaying like delicate reeds held upright by the barest of roots floating in water. Our intimate knowings with Him continued and began settling into a sound, a tonality of ecstasy that vibrated throughout our beings.

Then we gradually sank, descending again to the Mother. For the rest of the day we found ourselves curiously light. It was as though we were floating, seeming to touch down only for the loving contact. Flowers had appeared and bloomed during the occurrence; obviously, the energy present greatly quickened the usual growth sequence. Our animals were sleeker, softer, and so loving. Imagine, an equus wanting to sit in one's lap! But in the trying there was no crushing of flesh, despite its two thousand pentars. No, it was as though we were floating next to each other!

Osan still vibrated, her dear face bright as a light flash during a storm, and Danan's color covering pulsed with wide circular motions. Finally, the ecstasy subsided into a deep serenity, a peacefulness, and a thanksgiving. We sat, completely unaware of time. After the stars had moved through their night-track, we stirred and arose. Some of us had to be helped up, particularly old Eman, who couldn't move at all. We laughed helplessly and clung to one another. Then we started back, walking tall and touching occasionally, our docile beasts staying close to us, their love for us so evident.

We reached the city by midmorning. All the citizens came and gathered with us before the temple. We raised our eyes to the Holy Point above us, calling in a great voice: "*Azar, Azar, farnan abos enstamen!*" A bell sounded, deep sonorous and lovely. (There are no bells in this city.) We knew that the universe was here with us and we with it; and over us all was the great Spirit, the core of us, the gathering of all beauty and lovingness — our Azar, our Main Love, forever and eternally so!

THE MANNA

From the Mantiran records of 89 direns ago:

Never had the way been clearer or the fineness fuller. Alphon was summoned, and rose up like a god, saying, "Let us minister unto all the shore lands, since their leaders and warriors are away, and since their harvests and gatherings are failed. So shall we give them of our stores." Which we did; we gave to the hungry ones, the ones silently clamoring for life — life ever wanting more life.

And now the ghost of starvation lies across our own land, the land of the Mantira. The Zin have poisoned our crops and we wait for new ones to grow. The Zin, led astray by Carla, halted our growings, then retired in confusion, sensing the wrongness of their action. Their violation of the agreement is very evident.

It seems that Carla convinced them we were planning to invade the contact point. She had wanted to become our leader after Alphon went on, but Danan was chosen. After brooding awhile, she went to the Zin and incited them. Now she is in their land. How she can stay there we know not, for their ways are strange, their shapes repellent.

Carla's demands are many. She wants the ruler's wristband sent to her there in the land of the Zin so that it can be duplicated. She speaks wildly of journeying on into the Zin time frame, of finding a people similar to us and helping them earnestly. We fear for her balance.

We are now tilling and cultivating, encouraging the new crops to appear before we weaken.

(The patch is cut and laid upon the cloth, which quivers at the newness of the addition. We wonder, Carla, at your betrayal. You have the same knowledge of Azar as we do. You know that He does not approve of the turning away from Oneness.)

Without the ardor of Michael we are lost. Michael, our angel, with the cutting edge of His sword turned away from tender flesh, from trusting hands, from open eyes. He has long spread over us His mantle of white wisdom. May He guide us in this our greatest trial.

The grain ripens slowly. If Azar controls the rain we will survive. (Too much rain causes rot.) Never did we think such a thing as this could come to pass. Karma is obviously raging through our inner worlds, the karma of chaos. What happened in the so-long-ago? The purveyor is here, come to apportion the pain. The mills of the gods have ground slowly, and we are now eating the chaff.

So we investigated. Our seers contacted the Others, who looked into the old records and found the pertinent histories. It seems that it all began in a primitive era of the Gyptic land of Ramsa. At that period food was worshipped by the inhabitants. It became a religion. When the waters came down, grain was grown. When the waters withheld themselves, pain was known, the pain of starvation.

The land was ruled by a brother and sister, who are Danan and Carla in this living. The sister used food stores for individual gain, causing many starvings and ruining the brother politically. They are now born as Mantirans, and are again enacting the same sequence, except in reverse. Carla, who was the brother in the previous incident, is now instigating this crisis out of an unconscious desire for revenge. Confusing the Zin sufficiently to get them to perform the poisoning, she then fled to their land and hides there, issuing statements of bravado. Danan, who was the royal sister in the previous living and the promulgator at that time, is now the passive receiver of wrong action. Thus the roles are completely reversed, but the childish, selfish, arrogant motivations are the same.

Some of us wondered how Carla and Danan could have been so spiritually advanced within our instructings and worshippings and yet be carrying such confusion within. Upon asking we were informed that reenactments of this sort are sometimes withheld for long periods of time, until the participants are all present and the stage properly set. Then the enactment will burst forth, bringing consternation to the participants themselves, whose lives may have otherwise seemed spiritual and on a high plane of endeavor.

Many in the council were at first angry with Danan and Carla for having brought all of this upon us, causing such pain and sorrow. But cooler heads reasoned that we all had probably been involved either in the original incident or one similar to it, and that therefore this happening *did* fit us — it fit our shortcomings, past wrong actions, untimelinesses, whatever. We realized that we must allow this reenactment to occur, abstaining, of course, from joining its emotion and instead holding feelings of love and forgiveness. We knew it would not be over until we could do this with sincerity and trust, for an outward reenactment remains unresolved until it is inwardly finished in loving acceptance. We knew that only then could the occurrence change and conditions right themselves. Only then could the Others help, in whatever ways were possible, to alleviate our very real emergency — the danger of starvation.

Danan was in shock as old, old memories were activated and came crowding into his mind. Not specific memories, but remembrances of emotions: of resentments, guilts, and desires for gain and for victory over others. He came to us in turmoil, pleading for assistance, and we immediately placed him on the meditation of permission, an inner declaring of *"Thy Will Be Ever Done. May I Honor Any Occurrence, Any Appearance of Thy Sense of History."* This calmed him somewhat.

Time passed. We waited for the new crop, numbly accepting the will of Azar. The rain came — cautiously at first, then with confidence and beautifully controlled. At this point we were eating the trees — the parts that were edible, of course. The Holtar survivors talked of sending us supplies, but it was too soon after the Holtar Destruction; they hadn't as yet the fiber to accomplish this. The other shore people were in a state of agitation. Should they help us or should they enjoy the feeling of revenge for past wrongs, real or fancied? They had forgotten entirely our helping them so many direns ago.* They delayed, and our stomachs grew lean.

Word came that Carla, still with the Zin, had fallen into an insanity, a guilt-filled horror at what she had done.

The Zin were now appalled at their destructiveness. They also worshipped Azar, so forgetting His teachings was unbelievable. They sent a representative to make amends for their irrational behavior and to offer assistance. However, there was not much they could do, since their foods

---

*See the opening paragraph.

were not fitting for us.

We sent an emissary back to confer with them, to explain the total history of the incident from our standpoint and to suggest their looking into their own past. They normally do not deal with knowings of reenactments, and in the abasement of their guilt at first would not listen. We finally convinced them to look at their part in the karmic pattern.

Being of a different time frame, they were not involved in our original occurrence. However, it was shown to their seers that they had been part of a similar event in the far past, one in which they were almost destroyed several times by a rival race that invaded and laid waste to their lands. They had then decided that survival depended upon the use of destructive power. Diligently pursuing this power over a long period of time, they ultimately chose the use of poisonous substances as their final defense against the world around them. All of this remained in their history aura, a time-boil that was now being lanced.

From the records of the Zin:

We, the Zin, *were* in trouble, of course. Within our frame all was ill. Distress lay in our villages, with our women and children crying, frightened by the wrongness in the air about them. All of our hopes and predictions were invalid now, and we waited amid mounting confusion. We knew of no way to start toward normality until we were adjusted with the Mantira and until the wild woman was gone, but how to get her to leave? Must force be used?

All we can do is wait, wait in our solitude, our apartness, our heaviness from the past. Is destruction all we are capable of? Should we destroy ourselves? Must the Son of Azar visit us and tell us?

Michael was seen yesterday by Morled on the low hill, his sword flaming! The viewers of the Hidden say he is the overlord of the Mantira. If so, what will become of us? This morning Morled saw him near the triad of Azar, with his sword touching the lower of the three. Where can we go from here? What punishment is meant for us? . . . May it come now, oh Azar, for in not knowing, we stumble on in our usual ways, which are now meaningless. . . . Morled saw him an hour ago near the substance temple where we keep our protections, the powders with which we bargain for our security. We fear we are doomed! . . . Michael was seen by Morled just now at the door of the council chamber! Thank Azar he doesn't know of this secret anteroom wherein I write, writing to save my sanity. (The woman Carla's imprecations are now heard throughout the city. We suffer, for her plaints are high pitched, and our Zin hearing is especially acute in the upper ranges. If they would only take her back!) . . . There, a step on the threshold — it must be Morled — I must quiet myself. Ah, the door is opening, but why so much light? Is it from a flaming sword? . . . Michael? It is Michael! . . . Oh dear Azar, what shall I do? What can I do . . . ?

And he simply reached out, took me by the hand and led me to the council chamber where the others were gathered. We sat in silence for a while. (*Her* voice also was silent, thank Azar!) Then he of the flaming sword spoke to us, his words like music through the hall.

"You of the Zin, you poor creatures of the Zin world, with your substances of death, breaking the laws of Azar. Do you not remember what the Son teaches — that *all* is Azar, and that His all must be loved and protected? Have you forgotten that every person is the protector and guardian of every other person? That unfinished entities such as you are not to take matters into your own hands, for your judgment is faulty, your memory scarred by the confusions of the past. You must instead seek the council of Azar in your undertakings, thus learning and growing, becoming capable of making your own way.

"But this you do not do. Instead you continue destroying, simply destroying in your vain search for security. Know that the only security is Azar!

"Your present crisis has its roots in the past destruction of the Holtar, the burden of which lies equally upon you Zin, the Mantirans, and the Holtar themselves. It has become a part of everyone's suffering. It is true that the aggressors, the Holtar, had to be stopped that day, but there were other ways. The waters could have been brought down, flooding from Mount Aborah, or sleeping substances could have been used. But, no, you wanted to try the purple powder, for you had never seen it in use and were curious.

"The Mantirans, unfortunately, were more concerned with the end than with the means. However, they did give attention to the later karma of the Holtar, which is in their favor, and you Zin did request aid for the Holtar from the Overall, which is in your favor, and the Holtar have subsequently repented their invasion, which is in their favor. So I will tell you this: some of the Holtar that were killed those thirty-five direns ago have been working diligently in the laboratories of the Other Place, trying to find a way to help in this present crisis. Desiring to make amends for their part in the Destruction, they projected ahead and foresaw the possibility of this emergency. They then set to work to find a way of solving it, and have done so! They have found an ancient formula telling how to create a substance, a substance of sustenance, that can exist in both worlds, the Other Place and here. They are bringing this substance to save the Mantirans, and thereby absolve you Zin. So go now into the other frame and gather with the two groups on the plain where the Holtar died. For the points of your three karmas are to meet there and be resolved."

So we gathered our people, and with *her* in our midst traveled through the contact point, coming to the plain. The Mantira were there, having been alerted. Soon the Holtar arrived, drawn by some mysterious urging.

We all stood waiting — and then heard trumpets, trumpets in the sky! And across the heavens above us came marching the Holtar from the Other Place. But they were so different now! Resplendent and glorious, their eyes spoke of the far firmaments, of wondrous things, and their hands told of love and compassion, for in them they carried Manna, the Holy Bread of Heaven. They came in waves, their numbers were legion, and they held the Manna high and let it rain down upon the gaunt Mantirans, who sang with gratitude. They then bestowed the Look of Forgiveness upon us Zin and we wept with relief. Turning, they inclined themselves unto the Holtar survivors, who gazed upon their loved ones with faces of exaltation!

Then, making the sign of Azar, they vanished.

We departed to our own place, there to cleanse our temple, from then on allowing in it only substances that promote growth and provide life. The Holtar departed to their lands, full of pride and joy in the realization that their stain had been wiped clean. The Mantira, receiving Carla and comforting her, made obeisance to Azar and climbed to their plateau home, carrying the plenteous Manna. All, *all* of these persons were spiritually reborn, living now in the creative joy of His Love.

And Michael departed through the heavens, singing the song of Mar-ye, who is the Beloved of all the Angels.

ONE WONDERS

One wonders where the loveliness goes when anger sparks and quivers, and where hope is, when all is drear and dull. Why do the fair and good come to nothingness, within a frantic cluster of shallow fears and small deceits, and where is the glory that began so sweetly? What little deeds and spoiled connivings have nibbled and nosed it away?

It is still here, the glory, but covered a bit with dust from the stable. It waits patiently, with hands on the railing of destiny and hair in the breeze of tomorrow. Its feet, slender and well-behaved, are waiting to walk gloriously through the poplars of Becoming. Its energy, poised and adult, is like a bounteous maiden, reaching, with foot raised, to open the door, ready to step into the lighted places. We must never fear that this heart-striking wonder is no more; it is evermore, ever here. Noble and shapely, it crosses the lawn like a beautiful lad from out of a fable.

31

When the roadway is dry, the earnest and well-intentioned will again move toward the City of Light. By foot and by machine with wheels strong and adroit they will travel the silver road, lifting their eyes and sparkling the air with their knowings, and scattering the Fair and the True in their sowings. The Hum will return and we will again be gracious. Our breath will be clear and our touch certain. Violets will reappear and the honeysuckle will leave its hiding place. A sureness will come into the land, and we will again know our fair, our precious, our most dazzling Lord.

All tarnish will disappear. Faces will be brightly lighted, their shadows having slipped away. Mouths will be tender; with chins of hope we shall meet the new day and pay homage to it. Boredom will have shifted and labored over the wall. Dullness will be gone, fled through the lower openings, and trust will be under our feet. A clarity shall come and succor us, and show us the way to the sweet-breezed mountain land, the purple plateau of Spirit where the proud and questing gather and gaze.

The roadways of smallness, the alleys of fright, the tight lanes of denial — these will all be covered by the flowering vine of acceptance. The dull and unlovely subsist on resistance; accept them as a perversity within God and they disappear. They are but a vibration that has teetered off its cosmic course. Show them the bright glance of harmonious regard and they will pull back into their former balance.

Remember that all soilings are deviations from the original *Clean*, that all stainings are temporal coverings of the initial *Good*. These lesser conditions can always be nudged aside by clear viewing. Underneath, the pristine is eternally there.

So set aside the coverings and see the true and fine without blemish. Then the flowering will come. Vineyards will blossom, and trees will chant their wonder. The fine light will enter everywhere, pushing aside all muttering, all cajolery. The morning of the deep breath will appear, running down the hills, striding through the streets, crossing over the thoroughfares, sweeping all before it and spreading its ancient enchantment everywhere, all fine and glowing — and once again the planet will be God's!

THE ZALTEC

From Mantira we traveled east six kilims. We were looking for the Zaltec, an exotic race who were reputed to be in the area of Mount Aborah.

We walked slowly through the vegetation, through Azar's garden, enjoying it all, happy and free. We came upon signs of human habitation: *actual signs*, posted in the forest, saying "Welcome!" and "May Azar bless you!" and "Come along, we are waiting for you!" Peculiar signs; we knew not what to make of them.

Some of us were distrustful. "Always suspect too open a welcome," they said, shaking their heads dolorously. Nevertheless we continued. I was especially eager, for my grandmother had told me of the Zaltec. She had gone to visit them, and when her chariot broke down, lived with them for several turnings. Her eyes still glow at the memory.

We traveled on and came to a child, a boy. He was sitting

on an incline, waiting for something — for us? Some wanted to seize him and get information from him, but I held them back, watching the boy. He made the universal sign of welcome, then vanished! Frena felt he had slipped back into the forest, but I knew better. He had truly vanished. What power do the Zaltec have? Can we deal with them? Beginning to grow a bit apprehensive, I set my thoughts on Azar as we pushed on.

We arrived at a clearing where garlands of flowers were strung from the trees. In the center on a flat log were fruits and appetizing dishes in bark containers, apparently set out for us! How we laughed and crowded around, ignoring Frena's talk of poisons. And there was wine, a delicious thirst-quenching wine that made us clear-headed rather than light-headed.

After resting we continued. Later, as it was nearing dusk, we kept thinking we saw a light through the trees, a soft blue light that kept pace with us, always about twenty lengths ahead. Finally, we descended a slope, pushed aside luxurious vegetation, and arrived at the gates of the city of the Zaltec.

Awaiting us was a great throng of beautiful, dancing, singing people, who looked at us with trust and fondness — and with compassion, strangely enough. They drew us to the center of a square where tables of food and drink were arranged and put flowers in our hair, even Frena's, who protested only a bit. We then sat, and someone in a rolling voice began talking to Azar, telling Him about our visit and of their love for us; blessing Him and speaking in endearing terms, which we thought strange; calling the children to lay flowers at the shrine there and having them talk to Azar (nothing like our formal prayers!). Then they placed a small girl in the center of the shrine, declaring that she was now in the lap of Azar. She clapped her hands, crowing with delight, and everyone applauded!

After a long, silent communion, as they called it, the signal was given to eat and drink. And such food! Such loving attendance! Such bright glances and smiles! Even Frena mellowed. Afterward there was music and talking and finally we were shown to our resting places, where we sank into oblivion on soft, fragrant couches.

The next day we relaxed. We talked with the women and played with the children, the men being busy in the fields and shops. The land of the Zaltec was marvelous. Each blade of grass was different and had a glow of its own. The spell upon this land was enchanting and gave one a deep, happy feeling, a warm caring for everything.

The most venerable of the women was Merte, an older woman with eyes so deep one could get lost in them. She told us they had known of our coming, and had welcomed us in the different ways. She said they had even sent Pelin, her grandson, to greet us. When I remarked on his disappearance, she smiled and said something about his being a good student of the advanced teachings.

Then she began talking about us. She asked why we were so tense, and though I thought we were unusually relaxed in the balm of the Zaltec, I answered that it was our custom to have concern for the future: to be vigilant, do the correct thing, seize the right opportunity, protect ourselves from wrongness, and so forth. These concerns of the mind naturally encouraged a tension in the body, for it had always to be *ready*.

She looked at me piercingly and said, "Why do you try to take on the tasks of Azar? Don't you think He and His helpers are capable? Also, you're not letting your higher mind operate the way it should."

I asked her to explain and she said, "Don't you know that Azar has sworn to protect and guide His children during the periods when they are not truly capable of protecting and guiding themselves? That through His entry point (which is our higher mind area) He counsels us and informs us of what we should be doing. This is a training of us, for we are not as yet capable of perceiving our own good — Perhaps by the beginning of the next Age, who knows? With the small surface mind that we use daily, we cannot truly understand where we should be going, what we should be doing, and how we should be doing it. So why be stubborn, if in the trying we only fill ourselves with tension? Let us allow the teaching aspect of Azar to help us learn and grow. This is what we are intended to do."

"But how do we start?"

"By talking to Azar. He is your father and can be approached. Do so. Approach Him. Look at Seni!" She pointed to a child who was trying to fit together the parts of something that looked like a wooden vegetable strainer. He kept trying and failing, trying and failing. Finally, he paused and said something and waited; then his hands moved in such a way as to fit the thing together properly. Smiling happily, he rushed off to show someone.

"Did you notice that he was like you at first, struggling, determined to conquer, to do it himself, becoming more and more tense? Then he remembered his training. He asked Azar *how* and waited — and the movement of his hands came!" she smiled lovingly.

"But Azar is busy elsewhere!" I cried, amazed that she did not know.

"Ah, Azar *is* busy. But do you think He would create more responsibility than He is capable of handling? Would He start raising a family that is larger than He is able to care for? Actually, He has His helpers, His older children who delight in helping with the younger ones, for they love all of their brothers and sisters without qualification. Although invisible, they are always within call to advise and help. We use the blanket term Azar — and it *is* all Azar, since these older children are now integral working parts of Him."

"But if one asks Him something, how does the answer come — flaming letters in the sky?" (When I am uncertain I tend to be sarcastic.)

"It *has* happened," she answered with a smile. "Actually, the process is this: our point of contact with Azar is given the message from Him and filters it down to our surface consciousness. Now, this surface consciousness is still being grown, so the contact presents the message in a manner that can be understood. Perhaps with an involuntary hand movement, as in the case of Seni, or with a truth given in a fantasy or a dream or in meditation, when the mind is clear. Possibly a friend who is more open to guidance at the time may present what is necessary, or a stranger may say something in one's hearing that becomes the solution to the problem. There are many ways Azar talks to us, as you will find when you start listening.

"But now, come. Let us tour the community and I will show you how we live."

We walked and talked, observing the culture of the Zaltec. Their work buildings were of interesting shape, open to air and sunlight. Their temple was an enormous edifice with terraces and hanging gardens, more beautiful than any we had ever seen. We occasionally passed small shelters with people sitting quietly within, eyes closed.

"Meditating," Merte explained.

"In the middle of the day and in public?" We asked, amazed.

"Yes. To us meditation is not a secondary activity, indulged in only after the important tasks are done. No, it is our primary activity, our way of linking to Azar. The strengthening and expanding of this linkage is one of the most important of all activities. Only the caring for our bodies is as necessary. These meditation places exist throughout the city, in order that people can link with Azar at any time. Whenever they wish they may lay down their tools and step into the nearest shelter. It helps with their work, too, for they have more creative energy when they return to it.

"Here, we are approaching my favorite meditation place. Let us enter and be with our beloved Azar."

We sat with her, even those of us who had never seriously meditated before. Merte sensed their uncertainty and gave them a simple method, an easy way to approach their inner centers. I had been trained by my grandmother, whom it seems Merte had known, and I slipped immediately into my usual meditative frame, but with what power, what clarity! Merte later said that spiritual power builds up in the shelters and increases greatly one's own energy in moving toward Him. (In fact, a radiant figure appeared to me in the recesses of spirit, telling me I was to seek out one Hilin here in this community and study diligently some of the higher techniques he was aware of. This I later did, to my advantage.)

After the meditation we moved on through the city, awed by the beauty and intelligence of its design. The approach to living here was quite different from our ways. Structures were built for usefulness, not for the sake of tradition. There were stark new buildings placed next to mellowed older buildings, both styles valued for the manner in which they helped people live more effectively.

We retired that night in quiet amazement, feeling deep appreciation for the privilege of being here with the Zaltec, in the garden of Azar.

When the way is prepared and the chalice filled, the very air will shout with newness. Birds will sing psalms, and trees will chant responses. All will have arrived. The self will know the Self, and one of the completions will be here. The wheels will

pace themselves harmoniously, and the mind will be balanced. The organism will glow with the health of perfect coordination.

The body will move and sway in accomplishment, involuntarily and with delight. The eyes will well into pools of trust flowing down from the plateaus near the Source. The points of energy in the air will dance and form shapes and diagrams, then dissolve into laughter and excitement! The colors of the forces will swirl with energy, blending and separating in patterns of rightness.

Our knowings will touch and we will no longer need words, sounds, or symbols. All will be revealed and stand forth with the simple pride of existence. All movements of fear and hiding will cease; all desire to cover, to pretend, to dress up, will cease; all efforts to dominate, to influence, to change the subject, will cease. We will stand forth, both splendid and ordinary, with stars in our eyes and acquiescence upon our lips, our hearts, minds and souls belonging to Him, our own, our love, our Azar!

We remained in the land of the Zaltec for a number of turnings, all of us changing tremendously. One cannot breathe the Zaltec air without ascending somewhat!

We were now consciously living in two worlds. (Actually one, but seemingly two — the physical world with which we are so familiar and the world of the being of Azar, which is the world of contact with higher intelligence and Its knowings of truth and reality.)

To at last know what truly *is*! And not just to know but to feel and experience! Knowing higher truth gives this world a logic, a cohesion that it did not seem to have before. All is at last unified, and there is but one theme, that of children being grown by a Father. How wonderful to realize that throughout the universe untold numbers are being grown by their Father and His helpers! And not an abstract, impersonal Father, but a warm intimate One who can at any moment be contacted and felt. And to know that we are growing and progressing under a detailed Plan, the workings of which we are not as yet capable of understanding, a Plan that covers every possibility of action or reaction that could in any way affect us.

Yes, we are surrounded by provisions. We will, under all circumstances, be provided for. Azar's care of us is complete and total, for His intimate feeling for each of us contains all shades of warmth and love. We can fail Him, but He cannot fail us!

THE DIMENSION OF THE STILL

And so at last it was ended. The living only on the level of material forms was ended. The wheels were now operating properly, the glandular system was balanced, and the upper eye was open. Light appeared, amazing, brilliantly colored light that flowed and soared around us.

Our primary emphasis upon physical matter had faded. While we still were concerned with material shapes, our attention was mainly upon this world of flowing light energies. How can I describe the resulting state of our experiencing? Our forms touched the ground, of course, going through their usual movings, but our feelings soared on bands of inundating, circulating light, radiant light, joyous light!

We could see thought forms, since they also are of light: shaped light beams ranging from pulsating emotions to clear tranquil knowings. They were carillons of color, cascading extravagantly.

We traveled over many areas, experiencing the colors of the different places. The lower islands vibrated mainly with flowing pastels; the high northern areas were bright with flashes of brilliant, startling colors; and the middle lands were lighted with warm restraint, with wondrous combinations of rich tints.

After awhile, however, we began to sense that something else was present around us. We began to perceive, though dimly, an immobility within all of the shifting energies, a poised *something*, a quietness. We looked, wondered, curiously examined, and finally saw that we had found something new: a stillness! We recognized it as another dimension. We called it the Dimension of the Still!

Looking closely, we saw that within and around all energy was this Stillness, a state of being having no apparent movement, no pulsation; it was just — Still. A Stillness having as its main attribute an eternality that was without change, pulsing, apparently, at a much higher vibratory rate than we could ever perceive. Our breath told us that this Stillness was infinitely precious and absolutely necessary. We sensed that it contained, indeed was, the only *true* continuation of existence, that our previously held sense of continuation was somehow lacking, even somehow false and fraudulent. The Stillness itself is continuation, is itself the eternal.

Little by little we began to experience the ways of the Still. We found that somewhere within each of us is an area composed of Still "matter," if we may use this term, and that by tuning into it we become of the Still ourselves. All we need do is contact this area and, so to speak, fit ourselves to it. Knowing that we cannot perceive a thing without having somewhat of its nature within us, we realized that to perceive the Still we obviously must have inside of us a Still component, a Still place, a Still threshold, through which we can tune into this highest of dimensions.

And so we were aware of three, not two, levels of vibration: matter, called the physical; light energy, called the emotional and mental; and eternal Stillness, called the spiritual.

When we first began to perceive this level, we were amazingly drawn to it. We were struck with a longing, a homesickness for it. We saw that some crucial part of our nature had always been of the Still but had been inactive for mysterious reasons. Perceiving it, we longed for more and more of it, for we sensed that that was where all value is, all beauty, purity, and satisfaction. *And* all real love — the kind of love that continues as it is throughout eternity, that does not ebb and flow or appear and disappear, as does the love based in the finite world. For the elements of Stillness do not change. They have no desire for change, no desire to go elsewhere or be anything different from that which *is*.

This is because the Stillness simply does not need anything. Being complete, there is nothing for it to want. Its only wish is to participate in itself. Being the basic substance of reality, its only action is to expand, to encompass, to unfold.

Any point of creating we will be involved with from now on will be based in it, in Stillness. As long as we are in touch with the Still, we will partake of the feelings of the Eternal and be safe forever. Not needing anything, we will be fulfilled and serene, with an eternal joy in our veins. All that is there is here. We are, forever *are*.

TO KNOW ONE'S PAST

The plains of Miron are lovely in the morning light. Their hummocks are miracles of flowering trees and bushes and are inhabited by many small creatures of exotic nature.

Alphrana lived near a hummock in the eastern province of Miron. She was strikingly beautiful, her soul in her eyes and love in her hands. Growing things responded to her touch with eagerness, spreading themselves, opening and widening at her caress. Her feet were as fluttering moon-birds, running this way and that, pulled by love toward this tree, those plants, that animal.

She had made a rustic temple on the hummock, using vines as a roof to screen the sunlight. With bushes and trees as walls, she created a temple for her dear Azar, and would sit there for hours, perfectly still, communing with Him.

Shortly after the day of her maturity, Alphrana felt a discontent. She felt a need to discover the purpose for her living, for her being here. She sensed there was something

45

special she should be doing, so she asked Azar, and the next day in her deepest meditation He spoke to her, saying, "*My beloved, you are here to help Me. You are to feed My sheep, to lift up My lambs, to care for the fallen, the lost strayed and stolen....*"

So she went into the neighboring city of Ramar looking for His sheep, His lambs, and found there three people starving in a hovel: a man, a woman, and a child with stomach distended in hunger. She brought them home with her and fed them, slowly bringing them back to health.

Her mother, who had been out of touch with Azar for some time, was fearful, not wanting their lives interrupted. Alphrana quieted her and had the couple build a dwelling near another hummock, where the fruit of the trees and bushes would sustain them for awhile.

The man, Rolan, started a garden and a grain field. In the evening he would sit in meditation with Alphrana, and Azar spoke to him with the same message, adding that he, Rolan, would be the overseer of the coming ones, the ones to be helped.

Alphrana journeyed often into the town, bringing back unfortunates, some broken in spirit, some in body. She was drawn instinctively to those of good nature and open heart. Her feelings would keep her from the evil and the lazy poor, the ones who chose impoverishment as a way of life.

Thus a colony grew under the direction of Rolan. He was a wise overseer, holding meetings regularly and explaining procedures to all. That section of the Miron plains grew beautiful, with the people industrious and loving. Alphrana now taught meditation to all, bringing many into personal contact with Azar.

Knowing that all happenings are a result of former experiencing and are lessons, she decided it would be profitable for those in the colony to discover why their lives had brought them to their former condition of hopelessness, and why they had been rescued from it. She felt that realizing these things would enable them to make the desired lesson changes more thoroughly and to move on to new learnings more quickly. So she went to the priests at the temple in Ramar and told them of her thinking. They smiled and said they approved of her project and would help her. They then explained that these past-time factors could be revealed through meditational use of the milky-white stones by persons with certain abilities, and they commissioned Zerol, one of their more talented, to return with her, taking a stone with him. He would remain for awhile, seeking out persons with the special talent and training them in the use of the stone, which would remain in the community indefinitely.

So Alphrana returned with Zerol. The children brought flowers and saluted the strange priest with the fiery eyes and curiously golden skin. He later explained that he had been one of the Holtar marching through the sky on the day of the Manna, and his proximity to the sun had stained him golden — and that he had brought this condition into the present living as a reminder to all of the glory of that day!

Examining the people, Zerol noted the ones with soul-activated eyes, and chose three: Soren and Lenda, not yet mature, and Albar, a little older. Their training would take several turnings and be exhaustive, for their body centers would need to be opened and tuned.

Time passed and the three were finally ready to work with the stone. Albar was positioned before it and instructed to stop his mental processes and peer within, accepting anything he saw as valid. He cleared his mind, looked, and saw an enormous building swaying in the ocean depths, moved by the currents, the flow of the waters. There were fallen stones everywhere, with palace trappings and once-proud obelisks lying askew. He saw huge fish in the ruins of golden temples and crumpled vehicles standing on seaweed-covered roadways. He turned in shock from the stone, became sick, then collapsed!

Zerol supported him and led him outside into the cool breeze. The others gathered around and Zerol explained that Albar had just seen a former homeland, the last important homeland in which they had all been together. They and the other inhabitants had destroyed it by psychic wrongness, causing the land to be swallowed by the sea and all to drown in grief and agony. This land had been known as Atalanta and the ones here at this colony were former Atalantans who were now working out the karma of that experience.

He said there had been two factions there, the Children of Darkness and the Children of Light, striving for political supremacy. Unfortunately, the dark ones succeeded, and in their arrogance proceeded to ruin a culture that had taken five thousand direns to develop. Ultimately they destroyed the entire continent with their elaborate and ritualistic wrongdoings. Now many of them were here in Miron, being cleansed and changed into lighted children, into true children of Azar, the resplendent One, the glowing One.

Zerol further told that these Atalantan livings were the cause of the Holtar slaughter of many direns ago. Most of the Holtar were former Children of Darkness at that time, and the Mantirans, former Children of Light. That conflict had been but another chapter in the age-old battle between these two factions of that unfortunate earlier civilization.

Albar needed time to recover from the karmic shock of seeing these tattered scenes of former glory, so they waited until he had regained his strength and then began to work in earnest.

Zerol showed them how to examine the patterns of different individuals. When the one being examined was placed in front of the stone, his vibrations, plus a silent request from the examiner, would call forth scenes within the stone, visualizations of the states of being of his past livings. These would reveal his pattern of achievement and show what yet needed to be done. The person being examined could then make the necessary changes within himself with a minimum of fear and frustration.

The three alternated in their use of the stone, working around the sun, healing the memories of the people as quickly as possible. It was felt there should be no delay, that some great happening was impending, and that a certain readiness should be achieved.

> **To know one's past, the other dimensions of oneself! What a simple solution to confusion, for all confusion is rooted in the past. When all else fails — to know one's past. Suddenly fate becomes legitimate and humans are simply human, simply unfinished articles of life being grown by cosmic gardeners and at some point being harvested. They are pulsations of vivid energy patterns, being refined and clarified, always changing, becoming everything at one time or another, and learning all ways of thinking and feeling, all kinds of experiencing!**

All in the colony now knew much of their histories. They realized that the reasons for their being destitute here in Miron extended back to Atalanta, where they had ignored Azar and destroyed a land that could not bear the weight of their darkness. They knew that many lifetimes had been spent in other settings, each one providing movement away from evil and toward good. Now, in this living, they were to give up whatever remained of their psychic illnesses and step into the clear light of Azar.

They were at first appalled by their previous states in Atalanta, then relieved and even proud of their ensuing efforts at improvement. They saw their extreme poverty in this living as a final testing. Their acceptance of having nothing, without rebelling and taking from others, was a declaration of their readiness for the present experience and for its further unfolding, whatever that might be.

As Alphrana and Rolan gathered more and more souls from the streets of Ramar, they were led to those who had achieved this acceptance. Many other former Atalantans were undergoing the same test in that city and failing, their desire for material possession and status driving them into thievery, illicit dealing, even the taking of lives. These would need to go through yet another cycle of corrective livings before being placed in a similar situation — in a setting such as Miron, where a training colony would be available if they were to show themselves ready for it.

The colonists became aware, through the stone, of what specifically needed to be done to purify their inner natures. In most cases certain types of meditations were sufficient. With others there were hypnotic therapies by Zerol, with a few requiring a degree of reenactment of deeply entrenched psychic illnesses.

The past livings of Alphrana and Rolan were very interwoven. They had been brother and sister in three lives: in Atalanta, then in the land of Ramses the Gyptic God, and then in Mantira as Danan and Carla*. Now, in this fourth shared living, they had again switched sexes (they had to smile at this). Carla, who had caused the near-starvation of Danan and the rest of the Mantira during the previous era, was now born as Rolan and was rescued from starvation by Alphrana, formerly Danan. What a relief to know that the entire sequence was culminating and that now was the time to experience a major uplifting, a dropping away of lower ways, an ascending into new heights of spirit.

Each colonist, after several experiences with the stone,

_____

*See Chapter 5.

could, if asked, draw a chart of his or her lives, starting with Atalanta and tracing the cleansings and growings through following lifetimes. And oh, the despair of some of them as they looked back on groups of livings in which they had moved slowly, oh so slowly! This, however, heightened the resolve with which they now approached their purification periods. Zerol used esoteric techniques for quick, fragmentary discharges of the more stubborn karmic blocks, first draining away their negative emotional content and then letting the person see the dynamics in action. Once the dynamics were truly understood, they ceased.

These inner cleansings were reflected in the appearance of the people. They became clear-eyed, their bearing confident and at times unconsciously regal. Much time was spent in meditation. This allowed contact with the higher planes, from which energies were transferred by interested helpers down to the meditators.

As time passed an excitement began sweeping the colony. It was coming, glory was coming, the white light of Azar was coming. Alleluia, Alleluia!

The nights were warm in Miron, except for the brief winter season. During the warm period most of the people slept out of doors, soothed by the light from the stars. One night the breeze was particularly warm and caressing and most lay in a semisleep, reluctant to withdraw their awareness from the beauty about them.

Suddenly, a light appeared! Opening their eyes, they beheld a giant star sailing out of the east toward them and they heard chanting and saw Forms in the sky — white-clad Forms moving with majesty, accompanying the star. Slowly they moved, but with what glory!

They heard the sound of running feet, many running feet. Coming to join them were throngs of people who had awakened from their sleep and rushed out into the night, not knowing where they were going or why, but certain in their movements. Also there came others who had been traveling awhile, strong-eyed people with the stamp of purpose upon them, who had heard a call and followed it.

All gathered on the plain and watched as the Celestial Beings approached, accompanying the star. Then a great white light burst over the land and a figure appeared, slender, well-proportioned, standing above them some forty-five kilers — it was the legendary First Son of Azar! He had come to gather in this group of saved ones, of grown ones, of tall ones, ones ready for direct contact with the higher lieutenants of Azar, ready to be peers with them in the name of Azar!

The First Son cast a look of infinite sweetness upon the throng, and said:

"My beloved brothers and sisters, I, your own, greet you in the name of Azar, our loving Father. I have come to tell you that this is the time for your emergence into Spirit. On this day the hosts have come to touch all prepared souls, to bind them tightly to heaven, to certify that they are now among the brotherhood of helpers, that they have passed through the mortal mists and confusions and have come to the side of the light!

"Know that you all are now angels, earth angels. You are forever cleansed of earth-mist impurities. You can now move through the many regions of the universe and be fitting, for your purity will open all doors. You will remain here to complete this living; you then will move on to other levels of work, of glorious work for Azar. While still here you will do all you can to advance your brothers and sisters in these lands, the ones that are not scheduled this harvesting diren, but who hopefully will be at the next.

"Now, My Beloved Ones, know that our Father Azar will bless and keep you, and that my love shall be forever with you!

"Farewell."

He vanished, and angel voices rang in glorious song as the star and the Host moved off toward the other harvesting points on Earth.

All stood stunned for a long period of time, then began moving again, with star-filled eyes and smiles of radiant love. They mingled and shared sustenance, then moved away to their homes and their new work as earth helpers of their heavenly brother, the First Son of Azar!

PRAYER 1

Our Azar,

We pray that our usings are correct, and that our restings are seemly.

We pray that our scenes are enchanted by your helpings, and that our conversings are phrased and molded by your sweet tongue.

Help us to toll the right bell song, to weed the right flowers, to mural the right walls!

Our loving Azar,

May we ever seize upon your musings, your quiet hintings, your oblique suggestings.

May we bridle and mount our desires, and charge toward your light!

May we soar with your eagles, and arc with your lightning!

May we hark to your angels, and swim to your islands. May we float on your love forever, and never waver in the holy endeavor.

*May the skill of the Savior uplift and give favor, and may we continue to savor the flavor of **You**.*

THE ENCHANTMENT IS UPON US

The tangerines are golden, with juices sweet and running free. We pause and thank the Source. Our breath relates to Him for a moment, then resumes its pattern.

We know now where the automaton is. It is hidden in the routine of nature, in the earthly care of growing things. It is not within the being that truly knows the Enchantment.

That being floats freely. He has abandoned his usual procedures and embraced the New. The movements of his body, emotions, mind, and spirit are now anchored in the Fresh. The gale of enjoyment, the harvest of accomplishment, the heaped riches of spontaneity are proof of his newness, his free-flowingness.

In this state the atomic shifts are dazzling, the molecular particles moving with laughter and joy, chortling at their radical release from sameness. My heart has a new tempo, it sings a new song. (We have left the beat of the same beat!)

We move, and draw aside for newness. We rush, and pause for change. We deliberate, then shift to impulse. We are a jewel with many facets sparkling in the light, with colors alternating and harmonizing.

There are now no set rules, only permissions within the larger directives, the directives of love, beauty, and joyous exclamation.

O Father of enchantment, Mother of plenty, adopt me now by proclamation, that I may be legally severed from the Old. Lay upon me a striking robe of impulse, that I may cleave to your edict of glorious change!

We will never fear the well-ordered path, for its colors ever fluctuate, its direction ever changes. Its ways vary within its overpurposings. Its stability will quiver now and then. (We are pointed toward spontaneity whenever tremors come under our feet!)

Even the rock shifts with changing vibrations. It is ever new within its fine time-points of disintegration, which is its continued determination to move to a newer state.

Possessions change as they gain a patina of familiarity. They become new in their closer positions of intimacy.

We love, which is always a newness, always a shifting from within. The stream of adoration never runs the same course. It pulls from side to side, from up to down, from wavering to certainty, from quiet to excitement.

Never fill the container; let it fill itself. Then you will be ever curious, ever surprised, and ever pleased.

THE ROH

When the way was open we moved freely and simply. Fordas was the leader, and he called the turns well through the rocky, thin ground of Pardu. We were looking for the Roh, who was reputed to be the highest one in that area.

It was said that he never ate, receiving his sustenance directly from the cosmos. To never eat! What a glory, yet what a loss, for delicious food is one of the charms of earth living. It was also said that he never slept. What an amazement! Yet what a disappointment, to miss the sweet dreams of the upper self, to miss its tutoring in the night.

But no doubt there were reasons. Perhaps he was too occupied with the intimacy of direct contact to bother with lesser enjoyments. Well, so be it.

We kept moving, searching. The land was quite barren but had a warm feeling to it, as though it were waiting with anticipation for something large to happen. From a high point we observed a different glow in the air over one of the plateaus, so we headed that way, aligning our directional instrument.

Drawing near the plateau we saw animals sitting quietly, facing in the direction we were heading. They did not stir at our approach but became quieter, more separate from movement. Not only small animals but also large predators, all sitting together. I suddenly dropped to my knees among them, feeling a fierce love and companionship, and a hunger to face with them what they were facing. But Fordas pulled me to my feet, telling me not to change levels at this time, and led me along until I finally came back to my own way of being.

We slowed as we approached the lighted area, for we knew not how to step into the heart of what was ahead. We stopped and became still, still as though paralyzed, and a voice spoke, an enraptured voice heavy with feeling. It said: "Come, come into the circle, for you are ready, you are prepared, you need wait no longer." A light came toward us and waited as though urging us onward, and as we moved, it moved ahead of us, guiding us up and into the lighted area.

There a figure stood, a figure with cosmic eyes and noble bearing, a universal man! A man no longer limited to Earth, but using Earth only as an appearance point, as a place from which to manifest energies beyond measuring!

He opened his lips and a thunder rolled toward us. He said, "I am with the cosmos. I know and use its power to accomplish unending things. I delve the depths of infinity with my mind, and my heart glories in the splendor of the comets I ride with! I am free, free in the energy of limitless space. Come, I will show you how to join me!"

He looked at us, waiting. We were dazzled and ready to bow to him, but I wondered. I wondered and stepped forth, asking in a loud clear voice, "Are you under Azar? Are you the representative of His love, trust and generosity, of His fatherhood over all the creatures?"

And He replied, "I ride the waves of Hesperus and know the path of Orion. I weave the air and plait the clouds, and travel the curve of desire to far Parthon, having commerce with the builders there, with their pyramid shapes and their soaring stars that light the night skies. Come, you may go with me!"

But I asked, "Are you a part of Azar's family, knowing His older Son and His regiments of helpers, the ones He dreams through, the ones He loves through? And are you a part of His compassion, watching over His creatures and helping them in their distress and need?"

He answered, "I have no time to help the stumbling ones. I have left their condition and have grown into the power of the far-off stars. My Azar is busy with planets rather than with creatures. Come!"

Fordas and several others walked to him and stood with glowing eyes and proud hands. He took them into his chariot, which rose, encircled by fire, and vanished swiftly into the heavens, leaving a trail of droplets of energy, of tiny jeweled blazes.

The rest of us stood there, waiting, heavy with uncertainty. Finally a Voice spoke to us, saying, "*Go feed my sheep, go lift up my lambs, go care for the fallen, the lost, strayed, and stolen,*" and a sense of beauty, of pure being came over us and we suddenly loved all of our fellow earth creatures, not needing to understand them — just their being fellow creatures was sufficient. The air of Earth felt fresh and new, and we were certainly home — at home in our *home,* our loving Mother Earth with her many families of creatures. We took the animals into our laps and held them awhile, and they gazed at us with bright eyes and knew us.

We realized that one day we would travel the cosmos with glory, but that now was our time for loving, helping, and being one with the sweet earth that needed us as we needed it. Some day Fordas and the others would return to complete their lessons here, but their time would be behind us because of their having been drawn away. However, it would not really matter, for within the arms of Azar there is no set time, only related aspects and viewings.

We separated the frail animals from the predators so that when the influence subsided the small ones could run and hide. Then we began making our plans. We portioned out the needs of our city state among us, assigning sections: twelve sections (as there were twelve of us), each of us being in charge of one of the wedges of the circle of our land, to help the fallen, the lost, strayed, and stolen within that section. We would lift up all that needed lifting and anchor all that needed anchoring. We would pursue the good of all, knowing that we were working for His good, Azar's good, and knowing that His trust was urging us on, that His love was fueling our days and nights of caring and helping.

And we knew that we probably would be too busy to eat or sleep much, but that we would not be in need, for Azar's concern would sustain and keep us, and we would at all times be in His bosom, resting in His regard and knowing the glory of our sonship to Him.

A-mena.

THE PORGAS

The ways of the Porgas are limited. Their explosive breath is only for destruction, their tearing and rending are repellent to the sight. We must never let them multiply, never let them breed.

Put them away in deepest ocean and in darkest cave. Let the men of Talidon unarm the Porgas and sail them to the purple sea, where they can rest in endless harmony, and take their metal-senders to the Caves of Malar, where the lesser creatures can touch them in amazement.

And oh, let us use their energy to light the way to Altar, the highest state of Altar, where one meets Azar face to face and drinks the cup of bliss and ecstasy!

Come near, my luckless one, and share my robe. Share my house and gardens and I will make you my son, bequeathing you my groves and herds, for the way is steep to Altar, and I am called.

Let my flowers bloom each season. I shall be with Him, and He will show me His blooming ones in the valleys of the sun and in the mountains of the moon. I will see the golden apples and play the harp of heaven, and draw wine from the stars and hold their jewels in my hands.

Then I will touch the foot of Azalar, the first of all the sons, and He will look at me. Triumph will spring up all around, the singing in my ears will deepen, and Joy will come!

LET US WAIT FOR THE FATHER

The sun was heavy, hanging low toward the water. It was wide, round, enormous. Some of us felt it was an entity that should be worshipped, but Hanar did not. "Wait for the Father," he said. "Wait for Him that made the sun."

Then a figure formed in the clouds, a figure with white raiment and dazzling eyes, and some of us started to fall to our knees and chant "*Lehara Alach*," but Hanar said, "Wait! He has been made also; his Father is our Father. Let us seek the Father."

Suddenly a particle of light arced across the sky and came to rest on Elan's brow, and his face was incandescent. He began speaking wondrously, words falling gracefully from his mouth like sweet grapes from the vine. People crowded to ask his blessing, but Hanar said, "He is no holier than we; he is just being visited by the Father's light. Let us find the Father, instead of His appearance. We must worship Him directly."

So we sat and meditated. We stated in our inmost beings that we would wait forever, if necessary, for His touch; that we wanted Him, not just His creations, His extensions. We waited patiently, poised in a high meditative state with quiet minds and expectant feelings, and something began to happen. Lo, a deep stillness came upon us. We felt the Eternal. Some thought this was our goal, that this was the Father, but Hanar whispered, "Wait, this is but His mantle. Wait for His *personal* touch."

The stillness deepened, and in our upper minds shapes coalesced. Figures appeared, loving, glowing figures, and we knew they were feeling-seeing aspects of Him — His angels, His harbingers — and they talked to us with flowing words. Some of us felt we should bow to them and seek their guidance, but Hanar said, "No, these are His friends, some of His many beloveds; wait for Him."

For a long time there was only darkness and silence. We would stop occasionally for physical necessities, but would always return to the meditation and end in the same dark silence. We knew, however, that our Father could not resist us, that He could not refuse, ultimately, any wish of His children, so we were steadfast in our quiet asking, our genuine needing.

Finally He came.

A warm feeling arose and spread through our beings. It was motionless for awhile, then began swirling, increasing, moving within us, becoming very *intimate*. Our breaths caught in our throats, then assumed a rhythm of their own. It was as though we were relinquishing control of our breathing — actually relinquishing control of our total being, for we were being ravished, completely ravished by this warm, ecstatic, loving Intimacy! We knew It was Him, Azar! He was showing Himself to us at last, our own Azar!

We opened to meet His essence, and it was like catching sight of and becoming one with our own identical *twin*! We felt as though we were turning a corner, and would at any moment see our First Home, the one we had grieved for and then forgotten, but still grieved for during the forgetting. The essence kept increasing, and we felt that any more of the Father's substance and we would simply expire, simply die!

Then other awarenesses came rushing in. We saw how He is the world and the world is Him, and how His love for us and the other created objects is the great force of the universe. We saw that all that ever happened to us was right and needful in our moving in His direction, and that there had never been a *single wasted moment;* that *all* action is a movement toward this consciousness of Him. We realized that even the lowliest and most sordid of creatures are enrobed in His bosom.* We realized that we are in our true place as a part of His Whole, resting now, confident, aware at long last that we belong and can move and play and accomplish throughout His universe in complete safety and complete Love! And are now so close to Him, so deep within Him, so *full* of Him...!

Later we relaxed and quietly moved away to our homes to sit and wonder through the rest of the night. The next day we went about our tasks, but with deep eyes and lighted faces. We were people who had known a great ecstasy, who still knew it and would always know it. We knew that from this time on we were working parts of Him, that our lowest as well as our highest activities were equally sanctified. We saw that our raising animals and tilling fields were as much a caring for His Being as if we were in charge of the largest star in His upper white way.

So now we rest in Him.
So now we move, and do, and are . . . Him.

---

*Many feel that since we are in human form, Azar must be also!

TO OPEN THE HEART

Let me tell you of Elysius' march upon the Holtar. Elysius was the leader of the Nebunar, one of the shore peoples. Due to some fancied wrong, the Nebunar decided to march upon the Holtar and subject them to their will.

Now, after the Holtar Destruction the remaining Holtar had permanently discarded all weaponry, so the Nebunar were taking no great chance in attacking. Actually, Elysius was greedy for the fruits of conquest. He was determined to win a campaign and thereby perpetuate his name in Nebunar history.

The Holtar knew of the impending invasion, and conferred with their Mantiran advisors. After much thought, the advisors suggested a *very* radical plan. They suggested that the Holtar simply open their hearts to the Nebunar, letting all action follow from that — that they regard the Nebunar as coming to them for spiritual help; for, as the advisors pointed out, people don't invade others unless they *are* spiritually sick. And since all sick people ask for help if only by the fact of being sick, then the Holtar would simply be heeding a request of the Nebunar by helping them — first by caring for any of their physical needs, such as food and drink, and then by explaining spiritual law to them, which would aid them in the gaining of a higher ease and sufficiency.

The Holtar were quite puzzled by the plan the advisors were suggesting. They saw it as bizarre, even irrational. However, after much discussion and meditation they did perceive its logic; they realized its genius, seeing it as a tremendous testing of themselves. Their own growth could be enormous through it, but would it work?

"Only if you hold fast to the truth. And it is the truth that these people are spiritually ill and need help and that you have the good fortune to be in a position to help them, thus earning yourselves merit in the eyes of Azar.

"There are several things you must remember, though. Do not let their use of force deter you in your helping of them. And speak against any wrong action. If they try to pillage, block their path, for if you are to help them you must not let them commit further wrongdoings; they are wrong enough as it is. Just tell them you cannot let them commit crimes against their own God-spirit; that you are their brothers and if you are to assist them you must prevent any continuation of wrongdoing!

"And if they threaten to kill you, tell them you will do all you can to stop that happening, for killing is the sickest of all actions. But if needs be you will risk even that, for if you are killed you will simply go to the Other Place for awhile, and then come back here to continue your lessons, starting where you left off. Tell them that in trying to prevent their misdeeds you will be gaining closeness to Azar, for since you will be doing His will, He will be with you, and if any harm comes to you, will be there caring for you. However, if they do hurt or kill you, they will then have to undergo grievous consequences either now or in future livings, in order to purge themselves of the fruits of their wrongness. Indeed, the breaking of Azar's laws brings tribulation sooner or later, for one must be brought back, sometimes painfully, into alignment with the laws.

"Tell them all of this. It will help them to know the truth, and will warn them that they, the Nebunar, should think long and seriously before harming any of you, their brothers here on Earth."

So the Holtar went out to meet the Nebunar, walking freely, without weaponry, their hands carrying only gifts of food and drink. As they approached, the Nebunar drew up in battle rank, but the Holtar simply laughed and saluted them and kept approaching in a carefree manner — *they had opened their hearts*! They had achieved that most difficult state of consciousness, the complete reliance upon Azar!

They stopped just before the spears of the Nebunar, and their leader Orlo stood upon a talking pedestal and addressed the Nebunar soldiers, telling them all that was felt by the Holtar. He spoke compassionately and earnestly, with elements of humor and joy. He explained that his people had no weaponry and never would, for they were now following Azar, who loved peace and harmony above all else. When he stopped, the Nebunar looked at him blankly, completely puzzled.

In consternation the Nebunar officers withdrew to confer. The Holtar offered food and drink to the soldiers, who accepted eagerly, trying to keep their spears up and refresh themselves at the same time. When the officers returned and abruptly ordered an advance, pandemonium resulted, for the soldiers could not force the Holtar away without harming them, and how could they spear down unarmed men who were offering them sustenance? There were some incidents, of course, some damage to the Holtar by the more brutal of the Nebunar, but their more sensitive fellow soldiers restrained them and made them stop.

Finally Elysius laughed. He laughed cynically, for being also a thinker he saw the truth in the action of the Holtar, and realized the pretentiousness and childishness of his own behavior and that of his soldiers. Nevertheless, he had set his course and would continue.

Calling his men to a halt, he told them to make camp. He then conferred with Orlo and the other Holtar leaders, telling them he had the means, the weaponry, to pillage the Holtar cities and strip them of all accumulation. Orlo replied, "But we could not let you do that. You would be harming yourselves too much. The demerits you would gain from that action would haunt you for several lifetimes!"

"Then give us what we want," countered Elysius.

"No, we will give you gifts as friends give gifts to friends, but we cannot simply hand our substance over to you, for it is not spiritually proper that people receive large amounts of goods without having achieved the right to use them. In your case it would strengthen your tendency toward selfish gain at the expense of others, which would only increase the sickness we are here to help you with."

Elysius, angered and not able to bear any more of these truths, thrust his spear into Orlo's body! However, the spear was deflected at the last moment by Spirit and entered a nonvital spot.

The other Holtar gave Orlo the necessary aid, then massed in front of Elysius and told him with great urgency that he was earning for himself much sickness and suffering, extending well into the future; that as his brothers they must insist that he stop mocking his Father, Azar.

"What are you talking about?" He shouted. "Azar is the god of war and victory!"

"No!" They said. "Azar is the Father and Protector of all

beings, and He expects His children to treat each other as loving brothers and sisters. You have hurt one of your brothers, Elysius, and we as well as Azar are grieved with you. Oh my brother, how can you damage another brother's body so?" Confused and beginning to feel ashamed, Elysius entered his tent, where he stayed through the night.

The Holtar priests set up classes there in the fields, and their teaching began to interest the soldiers, who had been told little of the truths of Azar. They crowded around and asked questions far into the night. When the sun arose the scene was more a picnic ground than a battlefield, with the Holtar again bringing food and drink from their carriers and offering it with friendship in their eyes. The Nebunar were still confused, but beginning to realize that all of this *was* actually happening.

Their officers were despondent and feeling rather foolish. They finally went over to the class area and began listening to the discussions. The priests were telling of Azar's interest in all His creatures, and of the system of helpers He has set up, helpers that are always present and ready to assist. One of the officers challenged this, saying that Azar was too busy ruling the universe to be bothered with man's insignificant problems, but the priest said, "No, you are wrong, and I will prove it to you. Abran!" he called, and a slight young priest hurried forth. "Abran has a special talent," he told the soldiers. "He can hear the voices of Azar's representatives, the guides and helpers that care for us here. These guides and helpers are from the Other Place and also from the Higher Realm. They are invisible to us, but we are obvious to them; in fact, they can see into our thoughts and desires, which enables them to help us more effectively. So now, Abran, ask our invisible friends to tell us about this officer in such a way as to prove to him and the others that we are telling the truth."

Abran was silent for awhile, then began speaking. "His

name is Tabor. He is the son of Elad and Meka. His wife is Rosan, and they have two children. He secretly hates war but will not admit it. He swore to himself before leaving Nebuna that he would not personally take any lives during this campaign. He is about to violate that oath, for his inner rage is starting to build and will soon be uncontrollable. You see, he cannot stand being revealed as anything but a perfect soldier. He now is extremely angry with me and is drawing his sword to run me through in order to stop my talking. I am told that if he does this, he will probably spend his next lifetime as a chained oarsman on the great sea, one day being killed by the sword of a brutal overseer and dying in great pain as a form of educative retribution."

At this, Tabor, who had been trembling with anger and had drawn his sword, turned white, for all the Nebunar knew of the tortured livings of the oarsmen, who were considered the lowest of humanity. He stumbled away to a nearby hillock and sat there, shaking with fear and anger.

The Nebunar were impressed by this, but still remained skeptical. Elysius sat alone in his tent, trying to summon up the fever of conquest, the desire for glory, but instead kept remembering the words of Orlo and the feel of his spear being wrenched aside, away from its killing stroke. He tried to picture how he would have felt if it had gone to its intended place, and he cringed at the picture of Orlo lying irrevocably dead, for he had truly felt the brotherhood of Orlo's words, the concern and goodwill within them.

There was a shout outside the tent, and rushing out he saw three of his men tormenting one of the Holtar, cutting at him with their swords. The Holtar was trying to maintain his calm, but was obviously terrified as the sharp swords made small wounds in his skin. Suddenly Philos, now in charge of the Holtar, rushed up and thrust the terrified man aside, shouting, "If you want to injure someone, injure one that does not fear your swords!"

One of the soldiers drew back his spear and thrust it from ten paces away. It went through the body of Philos, who remained standing for a moment while he looked at his slayer with inquiring eyes, then fell forward in death. Elysius, sickened by this brutality, thrust himself at the soldier, shouting "You would kill an unarmed man? You butcher!" and began striking at him. Then he realized that he himself had tried to do the same thing a few hours before!

The whole camp was silent now, aware at last of their inhumanity. Elysius said, "Hear this, soldiers of Nebuna. We do not belong here. We are on land belonging to others and are guilty of crimes against these others, these Holtar, who have tried to treat us with restraint and compassion. We will at once return to our own land. There we will ponder our future course and try to discover what Azar would like of us, what ways of behavior would be pleasing in His sight. I no longer believe He would have us destroy and kill, for our victims are other sons of His and are our brothers. Somehow we must learn to treat them as such."

He then declared that the slayer would be bound to Philos' family, indentured to help provide for them during the rest of this living. But the high priest stepped forward and said: "Vengeance is not ours, O Elysius, it is Azar's. And Azar will provide for the family of His slain son. Let the slayer return with you and learn concern and compassion for others by serving in his own land. We acknowledge him as a son of Azar who will one day feel the same love for others that we feel for him.

"Now go in peace, men of Nebuna, and may Azar *open your hearts* and grant you an awareness of His Harmony, His Being, His Oneness, His Love."

The Nebunar departed.

HOLDAR'S PLACE

The access to the mountain was fairly well hidden from the high road. We walked to it by a roundabout way, not wanting anyone to see us and become curious.

When we reached the path at the foot of Holdar's Place, as the mountain was called, we paused and ordered our thoughts, for it would be dangerous to proceed further with an idle mind, a mind that could be opened too easily while we were passing through the first energy belt. Furla's belt, we later called it, because on that first day we were almost vanquished and taken over, being saved only by Furla's mind training.

When the force hit, the others staggered in confusion and I was hurled to the ground, senses reeling! Furla immediately switched to command state and told me with urgency to think of Ramsa, my protective spirit in the Other Place. I did, there was a struggle, then the weakness left me.

I got to my feet and we advanced, looking neither to the left nor the right, as the manuscript had instructed, just concentrating with enormous intensity on letting nothing in.

When we were through this psychic zone we relaxed a bit, preparing for the next energy belt. It would be the mental area, so we cleared our minds and lifted our consciousness up, up above the mental and into the White Light of Azar. Proceeding thus, we were not touched by the mind forces gathered at that point in the climb.

We then stopped and camped for the night, since darkness was coming. This would also give us time to stabilize before dealing with the crest of the mountain — Azar's womb, as people called it. There we would be entering the creative awareness of Azar, experiencing again, after untold ages, His primal creative force.

(It is said that this location remains from the far previous days, the days when there was a more open contact with the Source and His helpers. That it was, in effect, overlooked when the Open Stations were closed down at the beginning of this darker age.)

In the morning we began climbing again. We moved in the prescribed manner — to the right, circling around and up the mountain. Our pulses quickened as we passed a stone marker declaring that the areas we were entering were under the direct supervision of Azar's angels, who guard all approaches to the Holy of Holies at the crest.

The path, winding under the trees, was cool and pleasant. Myriads of flowers began to appear, some even hanging from the trees in garlands of color. Looking closely, we saw that they had been picked and woven together, apparently remaining fresh for long periods of time, sustained by Spirit. We began to see forms among the trees, white figures whose radiance reached out to us like fingers of help, beckoning us on. We trembled a bit, in preparation.

Walking toward the crest, we felt a pulsation in our eyes, and our feet lifted somewhat from the ground. Light filtered down as though through glare-shields of some kind — a rich light, not hot, but pleasant to see and feel.

Finally we walked the last few steps up to the saddles of Aaron, as they are called. These are an unusual arrangement of sitting places, formed by flowing stone upon the very spine of the mountain. We sat there in those naturally hollowed seatings, and it was almost as though we were in saddles, riding an animal called Earth. We looked around and up and down, and the view was unbelievable. We could see the two rings circling the lower slopes, the psychic ring flashing with brilliant reds and purples, and the mental ring pulsating with flames of yellow and orange. Above us the air was a warm light blue, extending into the deep blue of the heavens. Looking farther upward we could see forms floating on high, forms of white, appearing both human and angelic.

"They are the helpers," Daren muttered, mostly to himself. As we watched we saw two of the shining figures separate from the others and start downward, carrying circles of gold in their hands. Descending to us, they placed the golden circles above our heads, where they became halos. Then they touched us at our hearts, and we felt a thrill of joy shoot through us, almost overwhelming us!

They had us stand and join hands, and the spiritual current increased dramatically, showing, their thoughts flashed into us, that closeness among humans enlarges the flow of Life. They then arose into the air above us and held out their hands, and we could see and feel a flow of energy moving vertically down to us, then back up again to them — a rotating, living sea of foaming light! A light so joyous and wonderful that we became unsteady and had to lower ourselves to the ground.

Their thoughts said, "Return to your city and give of this

great love-energy to the people. If you try to keep it to yourselves it will dissipate, but if you give it to the others it will increase and flow always through you and you will one day be judged as true helpers, helpers of Azar!" They smiled sweetly upon us, then rose into the heavens, rejoining the other figures there.

We sat quietly for several hours, then with difficulty started moving again. Taking the path down the mountain, we walked as though asleep, so bemused were we by our feelings. Passing through the belts without noticing, we walked across the plain to the city, full of resolve and confidence, planning our service, renewing our dedication and radiating, widely and freely, our love.

THE HEALING CIRCLE

We have come to Tanivar, where the dates are moist and the corn bakes well. We tether our beasts in the soft, sweet clover. They are lowly, faithful, our servants, our friends. We break our bread, toast our days and praise our God.

We then start the circle, the magic harmonious circle. The Others join and mingle with us, raising and praising, singing with power. We give ourselves over to Azar, for He is the weaver. He plaits us, He braids our flowings and intermingles our pulsations, creating among us an amalgam of forces, a funnel of holiness, a giant ray.

Then His love comes down, and the funnel of holiness swirls and shifts. It opens at the top like a blooming flower — a flower of love and beneficence, of giving, of compassionate sharing, a flower needing a recipient to give to and enter into.

It rotates. This ray of holiness rotates and moves upward at the speed of Helat, flashing through the heavens, through the overshield, guided by the white Others, their robes gleaming in the warm spatial darkness. All shining and glowing, with eyes penetrating, they are looking for and finding souls that are needing; that are longing, wanting, and praying; that are hurting — souls who will receive, sweetly receive, petals from this guided flower of God! Souls who now brighten and sparkle and arise refreshed, moving out to continue their own ways, their own paths of service, giving the blossoms of their own rays to their own circles, their circles of embryonic gods.

And we, beautifully aflame with the flowing and the giving, sit in peace. We wonder, and occasionally breathe.

Full, still, and eternal, the All is here, sitting with us, at one with us, resting with us on the seventh day.

THE TEACHERS

The mutiny was prepared. At dusk the men in the lower level simply rose from their oars and swam toward the shore, never once glancing back.

The island was a paradise, with fruit- and nut-bearing trees reaching toward the sky. Almar, the leader, stood above the others and said, "My comrades, we are now to fulfill our destinies. We have served our fellow men long enough in the transporting of their materiality over the seas. We will now serve our own purposes. Let us know that Azar has placed within each of us a purpose, an activity to accomplish. Know that these will be actions that will serve others, for serving Azar and His Plan means serving others. Now let us rest, and then, in meditation, ask Azar what we are to do."

Which we did, and it was given me to build an obelisk, a pillar, and decorate it with the symbols of the Other Place. These symbols were revealed in meditation and were quickly translated into stone, Gar and Hamil helping. At last we raised the point of the pillar toward the sky. It was anchored well in rock, its narrowed tip pointing straight up into the realm of Azar.

Later, in the darkness a thin stream of light could be seen emanating from it and reaching far out into space. We felt that Azar was using it as a calling device, a signaling post. We watched it every night; the light never wavered as it extended out from the obelisk.

One evening we were amazed to see another beam of light coming *to* the first one from out in space: a large stream of light, meeting and pushing the first one back upon itself, the new stream then spilling down the stone pillar, cascading onto the mortar at the base. It gradually increased in intensity, glowing and pulsating, as a shape of metal from which the beam emanated appeared in the sky, approaching the obelisk. We were told later that the symbols chipped into the stone of the obelisk were of a calling nature, calling like-minded souls, beckoning to the brethren.

The shape lowered itself to the ground next to the obelisk. A section of it opened and two beings stepped out. They were as us in shape and were richly dressed and of obvious refinement, with intelligence and warm regard in their eyes. We made the gesture of welcome, and they came and sat in our midst. Their language was like ours, though strangely different. There were unusual sounds in it, so they had to speak slowly and we had to try to understand, which perhaps sharpened our reception of what was to come.

They were teachers come to teach the remnants of man wherever they were found. They go from place to place in the universe, called by the symbols which are given to seekers when they are ready. They explained that our service to other men as oarsmen and carriers had been long and honorable. Then suddenly something within us sparked, lighting a flame of necessity that brought about our abrupt departure and freed us for the next step we were now to undergo. They said we had gained much virtue in our serving — humility, steadfastness, self-respect — and were now ready for instruction in the higher awareness. They would stay with us until this was accomplished and we had moved on to our new condition.

It was not clear to us what the next step would be. The beings talked learnedly of traveling toward the spiritual plane, of expanding our horizons, of climbing the ladder of life, but these terms meant nothing to us. They finally looked at each other, laughed and said, "Forget what we have been saying. We wanted to see if you could still be caught in the trap of status words, of words sounding grand but meaning little. Obviously you have passed beyond that particular involvement. So now let us begin our work!"

The teaching started, and it *was* work. On the physical level we were given a complex combination of positions, postures, and breathings. On the mental level we were taught several types of imagings, of picturings, and were told what what their power could accomplish in the human world. On the spiritual level we were shown how to come into contact with our upper selves and through them, the Higher Realms. With these practices we gradually approached the Open Light. We were told to watch for It, and at times could see portents of It within us.

Our lower natures were rigorously examined. It was accepted that there were dark memories there, since the lower mind is the repository of the past, and we needed to establish that there would be no conflicts from these inharmonious factors rubbing against each other, so to speak. Some deep hypnotic work was required for some of us.

Soon we began to vibrate slightly and to hear a high-pitched hum, which told us that certain areas were being energized and opened for activity. This is done by holding in the mind the possibility of opening, then bringing all resolve and dedication to bear. The awareness then expands and encompasses the self (much of our training was about permission, the allowing of things to happen). Pulsation would then begin, and it was as though a number of energy wheels within the body were being spun by quiet motors. Once these wheels were active and in balance, their spinning could be felt by the innermost soul, the loving soul, waiting to one day burst open like a bud on a hypris tree!

The beings said, "The day is coming when your walls will open, exposing your hearts to the magnificence of Spirit. Until then be patient, and relieved that the way is at last clear. Continue as you are and glory will come to you, O beloved of God, precious souls, gleaming and sparkling in the compost of earth, dark, rich, warm compost, excellent for growing God souls.

"So let the book open, let the signals start, let the vibrations be felt. It will not be long, for the way is now clear."

Come, harbinger of the new day, the one reaching forth out of the welter of ones within the self; reach me a fineness, a largeness, a holy breath, and I will respond. I will open myself to the All, shouting forth in excitement, in exaltation!

I will then be One forever, Amena, Amen.

SO NOW THE FOG WILL LIFT

The bulwarks were down, and flowers were springing up in their crevices. The people cheered and sang with pleasure, for at last the long night was over. The stars had turned and brought forth a new era. No longer was the dark influence of Rebra to command Earth's respect! No, now the Triune of Alcazar was to hold forth, and all would be free and loving. The priests chanted their praise and the children danced with joy.

Jak, the overseer, was civil, barely. He had enjoyed the gloom of the previous era. His hands were seamed from too much effort, his face from too many tears. His words were full of grief and pity. He would not change, so he was given a small farm on the outskirts and told to settle there. His successor was Altha, who had striven mightily against the previous darkness.

Altha immediately decreed amnesty for those imprisoned for crimes against the government. She felt they had suffered enough for what were simply outbursts against the grayness of the times. And she freed by decree all indentured servants in households of civil leaders, feeling that they, the leaders, should be examples of charity and compassion. Oh, there was grumbling, I tell you, for the leaders, used to much service, would now have to do without.

Altha called us together and told us of things to come. At one point she said something curious. She said that emissaries had contacted a people to the north, the Mantira, who would be sending teachers to instruct us.

"Instruct us in what?" We asked.

"In the ways of the Spirit." She said.

"What is that?"

"It is the higher part of our beings, and if recognized and attended to will lead us into new and glorious adventures! Spirit has the power to overcome negative eras like the last one, for It can even counter heavenly influences. Its authority comes straight from Azar, who will listen and help in keeping our ways successful and happy."

"How strange," we said. "Does this mean we no longer need to go through dark periods? That we can learn to command our own state, and keep ourselves open and bountiful?"

"Yes," said Altha. "These people, the Mantira, will bring us a new knowledge. A knowledge of a power that has existed from the beginning of time, the power of the higher self. We will listen and follow these teachings. They will help us find peace and serenity, and confidence in ourselves and our universe, the universe of Azar!"

So now the fog will lift, slowly and hesitantly. The oversoul will burn it off with its rage of energy and love. The human entity is no longer an embryo: it is a full-fledged, lusty child, ready at last to cope with the sun, no longer needing the protective dampness of the fog.

We are to be taken out of the greenhouse and into the light!

Alleluia!

THE SPLENDOR

Never had we known such splendor, such magnificent heraldry. The moon was lying low on the horizon and Azar's stars were overhead. Trees trembled slightly in the stillness. Then the wind arose and shook the flowering bushes, and the wheat in the meadow whirled and spun on its stalks.

We looked up and saw a mass of color moving down from the sky. Mostly purple, it was as a small cloud floating gently to earth. It touched down and two forms came from it, a young man and woman dressed in silver and gold. They were obviously not completely human in form, for their bodies shimmered and were somewhat vague in outline. We realized they were spirit beings, using earth forms as a focal point. The stopped twenty paces away and the man spoke to us, saying: "People of Mantira, you who are here questing for truth and honor, we give you greeting. We have come to enlighten you, to give you a glimpse of what happens when souls grow beyond the earth experience and move into the Higher Realms. We two were soul-mated beings for several ages, when Earth was younger. We incarnated over and over, learning our lessons and slowly growing to maturity. We were a part of magnificent civilizations and of primeval cultures. We saw all, did all and were all. Finally our long Earth tour was over, and we graduated to one of Azar's higher schoolings.

"We are now of another vibration, a finer vibration, which can command at will the forces of Earth. Although our home is on a higher level, we can descend again, constructing forms to appear in and creating spectacles of play and worship — which are actually the same!

"We do this to aid in your enlightenment, to verify for you the going on from here, and to show you the freedom and ability you will have when you graduate from this planet and move on to the Higher Realms.

"Now watch. We will give you an example of how we emancipated ones occasionally enjoy ourselves here on Earth."

He gestured, and a bank of trees rose into the air! Dipping sideways in rhythm to a singing we began to hear, they moved ecstatically above us. Water from the river ascended to lodge on their leaves and branches, and lights appeared in the sky glowing down upon the trees, turning them silver, gold, and purple, the drops of water glistening and reflecting like sparklets of energy.

Our horses lay down indolently in the field and permitted a host of small creatures from the forest to clamber upon them. They were the nature helpers of Earth, small, stocky and bright-eyed, in miniature human form. At their command the horses came to their feet and stepped up, up into the air and went galloping over the sky, going every which way, the small ones laughing and the horses neighing with pleasure! Our steeds ran vast races through the reaches of the heavens, finally coming to rest beneath the burnished trees and standing fresh and confident, looking down at us inquiringly.

The woman said, "These helpers, sometimes called the small ones, are on their own growth path. They are from another solar system, and work here at times to learn service. They are occasionally given this kind of recreation, for they are steady and faithful workers."

Then a tall being appeared, stepping from the fronds near the river — a beautiful woman, with vines growing about her. She drifted upward, the river reeds growing up with her and surrounding her on her couch of air in the open sky. Small animals ran up the reeds and nestled in her lap and birds flew up and sat upon her shoulders.

"She is a symbol representing the fecundity of nature. We are projecting her in this form to help you see the beauty of the earth. Now watch and see how the growing things react to this focal point of nature energy!"

The trees surrounded her and bowed, and the horses formed a circle around it all. The wind moved through her hair, floating it out into the night, and owls with loving eyes flew to her and stood as sentinels at the four inner corners of the group.

The stars seemed to bend nearer, and suddenly there were hosts of lighted beings in the sky moving toward us, wheeling in rhythm. A humming started and spread up the scale, forming a shimmering melody that charmed and soothed us.

He said, "This is one of our ways. At times we form these spectacles, which are a loving, playful salute to our own dear Azar.

"And now look! You can see Earth reaching its love up to Him, while the higher hosts chant their praises! This demonstrates to you that once physical thralldom is removed, all creatures sense the movement of Spirit and bow to It.

Look!"

We saw that the horses and animals and trees — all of the earth creatures and objects in the sky — were making obeisance to the spirit forms above them, and we did so ourselves, without thinking. The higher forms were bowing also to a Something above them that we could only sense, not see. All of these held their poses while an indescribably glorious sound swelled and filled all space. They then relaxed into a quiet serenity.

The man said, "You are a loving group, strong in your trust of Azar. May this seeing strengthen and fortify your resolve to move toward Him and thereby join us in the Higher Realms. There are many places there, with much to do and further distances to grow.

"And now all of these beings and growing things will return to their original states. For in no way do we interfere with the growth patterns here."

He gestured, and the horses returned to the meadow, kneeling to let the small ones dismount. The trees sank back to their clinging places in the earth, and the female nature figure descended, then expanded and turned into points of energy that flashed off into the meadows and valleys around us.

"Remember this seeing and honor the grace of its being bestowed upon you. Tell the others of it to help them believe. Our love to you."

The man and woman reentered their cloud of color and ascended back into the heavens, surrounded by the shining hosts whose voices rang in praise of the Creator and His creation!

THE DARK ONES

When Hora split the evening sky and Elas brought forth the celestial flowering, we complained and felt no love for the invaders, the homeless ones looking for living space, for gardens to grow in. Their lands had been shaken by the fires within Earth and were now uninhabitable. Their faces were dark but hopeful, their ways joyous but sense-laden.

Where could they go? Where could we put them? We talked of this, discussing the ways, and finally came to a conclusion. Each of us would give one part in ten of our lands to these dark ones. We would let them live in our midst on these parts, becoming adjusted to our agricultural ways, the ways that fit this subcontinent and its peculiarities. Then when they were sufficiently facile we would help them start in the Moran valleys, where the Nebunar had tried and failed. For these ones had a persistence that could conquer the Moran conditions. Their hands would move over the land, shaping it, quieting its agitation, bringing it to peaceful cooperation.

We would then formally ally with them, these homeless ones that Azar had brought to us, these drifters on the sea of chance. We would encourage their confidence, for they were darkly beautiful and full of shadowed grace. They knew that Azar loved them; their eyes were bright with trust.

We vowed there would be no disagreement during their occupance of our corners: no resentment in our young ones, no heated movements or campaigns of dislike, for Azar is mindful of mercy and values compassion. We would welcome them and give them of Azar's love, never permitting the sickness of color hate nor the fear of differences.

We would simply feel happiness at Azar's prodigality, at His enjoining of His sons and daughters to be clothed in differently colored surfaces, with different shades of amber in their eyes and different sorts of felicity in their hands.

He is all-wise and all-loving and His variety of creatures is extremely commendable!

THE ZAMBAR

When the horror was done and steps to alleviate it were taken, Carla found that Danan's body was peaceful and that the buildings could be reconstructed. The force had been sudden and overwhelming. Where had it come from? What had prompted it?

Obviously there were enemies, enemies of the Mantira. Carla called the seers, who began probing the incident. They found a cloud of darkness to the east where the metal city had been many direns ago. The seers could not penetrate this cloud, so the temple high priest was summoned. He was asked to contact, through his mediumistic processes, the Other Place and ask for help in discovering the perpetrators of the destruction. He did so, and was told that on the former site of the metal city were curved buildings without windows that were inhabited by members of a race from the farther east, a race that lived away from the sun, to which they were sensitive due to the radiation wars of the past (the firing of the Porgas). He was told that this race was proud and coldly scientific, their industry given over to acts of destruction. They had already affected several areas of the continent.

Their way was secrecy. Living only indoors, they had developed instruments for scanning the outside, and their interest and amusement was to observe a scene of activity in another land and to interfere, using their destructive rays. They enjoyed watching the destruction itself and the varied reactions of those in the environment. They had centered their rays on our temple area at a time when Danan was in meditation. He had been killed, as had a number of the temple inhabitants. The high priest, being elsewhere, had been spared.

They were the Zambar, from a land previously known as Indi. They were an unusual mixture of races, a curious amalgam of bloods. Because their emphasis was only on the mental, their spirituality was blocked off, as were their physical pleasure areas. Their only interests were science and games of destruction.

Their psyches had been fairly well-balanced at one time, but the pressures of the radiation wars had led them to compress themselves, being active only in the lower mental areas. The unconscious frustration within the other parts of their beings was causing them to be destructive — ostensibly to others, in reality to themselves, for they were completely unhappy in the deeper parts of their natures and hated what they had become. We could not combat them physically, for we had no science of destruction. Our efforts could only be on the psychic and spiritual levels.

Carla was our leader now. She had grown much in the period since her misadventure with the Zin, and it seemed only natural that she assume the leadership of the Mantira — although, curiously, she did not seem to crave it as she had before.

At a hastily called meeting of the Council she informed us that she had been studying some of our more unusual temple techniques, and now wanted, in this emergency, to use one of them. This particular technique would enable her to leave her physical body here, resting, and with the help of the high priest and his connections in the Other Place, go in her invisible soul body to the city of the Zambar, where she could come to know the inhabitants intimately. This procedure was known to be dangerous, but she insisted that with the appropriate help she would be safe. We of the Council gave our permission, reluctantly.

Carla started her activity. She would go to the Zambar for a period of time, then return to use her body for awhile to keep it operating properly. Looking thoughtful, she said little when we saw her, which of course raised our curiosity dangerously! Finally, after a particularly long period there, she called us together and spoke thus.

"The Zambar are beautiful, in a rather evil way, but are internally very unhappy. They have closed down all feeling centers containing warmth and love and are operating only on a cold, impersonal, mental level. They have the capacity to completely destroy us or any other nation.

"Fortunately, they do not wish to do so. It is, rather, that the playing of games is fashionable with them. They try curious destructive ventures to elicit unusual reactions from their victims; the more bizarre the reactions the more prestige the elicitor gains. They admire a type of skill, the skill of not killing as such, but of seeing how long and furiously their victims will wriggle while impaled on pins.

"The ones working on us at present speak of their activity as the Mantiran project. One Royl is in charge, and wants to achieve fame among the more disdainful members of his society.

"They are extremely interested in our reaction to their recent destructive thrust. Through their instruments they have watched the burials of those killed and the rebuilding of the temple, but they have not seen the confused and frightened efforts at readying weaponry that they expected. This puzzles them. They, of course, are not aware of our activities of inquiry — the council meetings and my trips — for these are hidden by a psychic screen arranged by our high priest and his associates. They have no idea we are watching them, for their seeing is done with metal instruments, and perceiving none of such here, they assume we have no means of observing them. Royl is planning another force thrust into us, which will cause earth tremors in places. They rather childishly enjoy watching buildings fall and people panic.

"Now, our only possible reaction must be to destroy, so to speak, their artificial self-balance. We must find a means of altering their cold, closed personalities, of prying open their psyches and reactivating the other parts of them. They are quite sick and, if they continue as they are, will one day fall victim to the flesh-changing condition which is the usual outcome of such feeling-area suppression.

"After studying the matter thoroughly, I propose that we work on Royl with the following technique. We will project to him stimulations of the main area that is closed off, the spiritual area. This area is being held in check artificially, but will respond quickly if we are skillful and furnish energies that will bring about a natural opening up in him. Poor thing, he will soon be so different from his associates!

"We will start by projecting a certain imagery to him while he is sleeping. This imagery will definitely connect with him, because it will present a view of Royl as he would be if he were spiritually open. An image of him "lighted" spiritually, so to speak, of him with a glow of love and compassion. We will project with it a request that the dream constructor within him take this spiritual reality and convert it into a dream symbology that will fit the dynamics of his surface mind, impinging upon it deeply enough to haunt him after awakening and make him feel a need for the qualities presented in the dream. As a result, his spiritual area will expand and become outwardly active. (His contact with this part of himself has become weak from neglect.)

"His upper self will cooperate with all of this as long as it is of benefit to Royl. Our contact with this self will be arranged through our connections with the Higher Realm. The beings there are quite enthused, in fact excited, for this will be the first time this way of opening a human will have been initiated here by other humans.

"You see, change imagery of a being is usually sent from either the Higher Realm or the Other Place. However, it is felt that an imagery transference originating here will be extremely effective and will move us (we poor misguided, pained ones) even more quickly toward spiritual normalcy, thus helping to open the planet and release it from its subjugation to the illusion of separateness."

The plan seemed so ingenious that we started with it immediately. The temple priest and his workers, using their developed psychic training, sent the spiritually energized projections to Royl — projections of him as a fully activated spiritual being, surrounded by the white light of Spirit. This was done for three consecutive nights, with Carla in Zambar observing. After the first night Royl looked thoughtful; after the second he seemed uncertain; and after the third he was definitely disturbed.

He told one of his intimates that his dreams of the past three nights were bothering him greatly. They were alike, he said. In each, a beautiful woman with incandescent eyes held out her hand, offering him a glowing something, a jewel, it seemed, but he couldn't bring himself to take it. Instead he put his hands behind him, as he knew they were soiled and dirty and he was ashamed for her to see them. His friend listened to this cynically, laughed and remarked that perhaps Royl should wash his hands before retiring. He then went on to remind him that it was time for the next step in the Mantiran project.

Royl, however, could not concentrate on anything but the dreams. He kept seeing the shining jewel and sensed that it was connected in some way with the scenes of the Mantiran people he had viewed in the past. He assumed there had been one like it in one of them, but upon again viewing the scenes in the chamber of records, he could see no such jewel. However, there *was* something, and he began to realize that the grace of the people of Mantira had a haunting similarity to the dream itself.

He thought about this, then dismissed it as of no consequence. A few days later he was more or less back to normal and working once more with his associates to calibrate the ray penetration necessary to achieve a small, localized Mantiran earthquake.

So again the temple priest and his associates projected spiritual imagery to him, and again for three nights Royl dreamed. This time his "dreamer" converted the energy into visions of an older man dressed as a prophet or hermit standing in a wooded setting and holding out a cup of flowing, sparkling water. But Royl, starting to reach for it, drew back in horror, for he saw that his hand was covered with blood!

Again three dreams in three nights, the scene being somewhat different but generally the same. Royl was quite distraught by now. The flooring of his life was giving way, leaving him hanging precariously over the ruins of its foundations. He knew instinctively that he could not tell this to any of his own group of friends, so after looking around, he approached an acquaintance named Elsed.

Elsed had always remained apart fom the Zambar mainstream. He spent his life immersed in the study of old books and paintings, and was an object of good-natured scorn to the knowing. Royl visited him and told of the dream sequences. Elsed, smiling quietly, showed him a drawing in an old book, a woodcarving of a regal-looking man holding out a cup of water, offering it to passersby. He explained that this was a universal symbol used throughout the ages of man and that it represented the efforts of the enlightened, wherever they were, to give the water of life, the refreshment of Spirit to all who thirst. He showed him other drawings and read to him some of his own translations of their scripts. He said it had always been stated that man is composed of four parts — the physical, the emotional, the mental and the spiritual — and that when these do not work together the person will be out of balance, in time becoming sick. He said he had long known that the Zambar were unbalanced. This was first brought about by the suppression of all within their natures but the mental; they then moved into a further degradation by bringing destruction to others. He explained that the first principle of our being, as formulated by the spiritual part of us, is to never harm anyone or anything. He said that destruction is a perversion that can come about only when an entity is seriously out of balance. He then went over all the dreams with Royl, explaining them minutely.

Royl was in complete turmoil, for many of his society's standards of behavior were being declared unfit. He went home and that night dreamed that a girl with grace and beauty came to him, and with a cloth and a bowl of water gently washed the blood and soil from his hands. He arose greatly relieved, for he knew this meant that his spiritual nature was now awake and active and telling him that he could become clean.

The very thought of the Mantiran project was distasteful. He felt its crudity, its aberration. He discussed all of this with Elsed and gained a greater perspective. He finally cancelled the project, retiring to his home for self-examination and the study of Elsed's books.

The Mantira were well-pleased with this when Carla reported it in detail. Their plateau was saved for awhile. However, after much thought they concluded that a larger effort was needed, that the same approach should be used with the other Zambar leaders. Carla picked out the five primary ones, and the dream technique was started with them.

And so they continued, working on this one, then on that one. The Zambar leaders gradually changed. They became thoughtful and were more often silent; they began to enjoy music, to read better literature, and were, upon occasion, actually kind. (Also, they never reassigned the Mantiran project.) Although the mass of people tended to remain the same, they slowly began to follow the new ways of their rulers.

Gradually over the following years, the souls of the Zambar expanded and grew. We had a permanent staff working on them — without their knowledge, of course. They simply assumed that their culture was growing and evolving through its own energies. Actually, the bulk of the energy for the change was supplied by the ones in the Higher Realm. It is supposed that this is always the case because, for one thing, they are nearer the genesis of energy and can channel it more easily.

Finally the day came when the Zambar outlawed the destructive use of the rays. In a decree handed down from their High Council it was stated:

"People of Zambar: For a vast amount of time we the Zambar have used our force rays in whatever ways and whatever places we wished, always affecting less capable people. These people have been

our outlets, our experiments, our victims. This is to stop, for we now realize that they are our brothers and are to be treated as such. No more shall we gain our sport at the expense of the less formidable. We now freely accept responsibility for our fellow men. We will help rather than use, and aid rather than abuse.

"Let this be forever so, forever true. And may we now begin to rest in the bosom of Azar, the high One of the Universe, the only One of All!"

We must remain in peace,
    under the glare of the sun,
        under its umbrella of solar rain.

We must remain in joy,
    under the flash of the comets,
        under their tailings of fire and pain.

We must remain in wonder,
    under the shine of the moon,
        under its heavy emotional drain.

We must remain in love,
    under the glance of Azar,
        under His widening spiritual stain.

THE VESSEL OF THE MIJAKS

Light is awake now and descending upon the wayfarers. It is pulsating and cascading downward in increments of fire, with knowings broad, vast, and unending.

"Our Father, we savor your flame reaching toward us, and we open our arms."

The light from the vessel reached the islands. It cut through the fog abruptly and touched the islands. The inhabitants peered upward, holding their palms together. With a loud clap of reverence the vessel of the Mijaks descended and came to rest on the northern promontory. The people walked toward it slowly, pausing occasionally to utter short phrases, as though counseling each other as to behavior and stance. Arriving at the vessel, they hit upon it with a staff. The door opened and a being stepped out, covered with a strange, inflated wrapping, his head protruding and surrounded by a transparent bowl. Mechanical words issued from a round object on the front of his covering.

"Children of Azar, may the heavens grant you peace and surcease from the tragedies of the great radiation explosions, the desecrations caused by the firing of the Porgas.

"May the ways of the Opened Man soon be yours.

"I bring you an object that will speed your recovery from the shape-changing influences. This object will purify and calm the outraged linings of your sweet bodies, which will then merge once more with the life currents, no longer revolving with a destructive force of their own. Their feeling points will subside from strained rebellion, allowing them to ripen naturally."

He brought from the vessel a device mounted on three rods with a round globe at the top. There was an extension reaching out from the device, and when he pressed on the end of it, the globe began to glow with a penetrating blue light, a light that covered everyone present and seemed to enter into the interior of their bodies. Faces softened, hands quieted, and a curious stillness enveloped everyone. Nothing could be heard but an occasional sigh of relaxation.

After awhile he again pressed on the extension and the light faded. He said: "Every day you will assemble here and press upon this extension, bringing to yourselves this light. Then after a length of time such as today, you will press again to halt its glow. This illumination will heal your bodies and change your lives, freeing you of the fears and sadnesses that haunt you now. When I next come I will not need to wear this covering, and I will take some of you back with me to visit my lands so that my people may praise and thank Azar for your delivery from the sickness.

"We all will then help the ones that caused the explosions. By devising a means of contacting them in the Other Place, we will start their healing process by helping them purge their destructive power-seekings. Then all will dwell in peace once more."

He reentered the vessel, which ascended quickly and silently. The people remained motionless, still experiencing the easing of their bodies by the blue light and still feeling the hope and comfort of the words just spoken by the one that came to them, the one concerned for them, their older brother, one of the older sons of Azar.

"And His love shall be brought to you and make you whole again!"

The intuition is coming. The ways of awareness are fast approaching, for time has speeded and discovery is near.

We will regain our lost sensings, our knowings of the Way, the Plan. Love will open our centers of perception and we will see, flowingly, the reality of it all.

And the movements of the mind will deepen and broaden, rising up in knowings that are of instant magic and utmost certainty.

THE LOST MANTIRANS

We looked through the shapes and saw Zarin. He was standing at an angle to the jewel, the magnificent jewel of our people, the Mebora. He was obviously sending his thought to it, in an effort to receive a communication. This is what the jewel is for. It connects with other intelligences in the universe, and their thoughts come back through it. It is usually red, but changes color when in use.

Suddenly a violet ray shot from the jewel. It expanded and seemed to penetrate Zarin. He staggered and braced himself as the violet poured into him. It then did a curious thing — it looped out of him and reentered the jewel! It is a rare occurrence for the jewel energy to complete a circle through an asker.

Zarin lowered himself to the floor, trembling. He opened his mouth and melodious sounds issued forth. I gestured to Roma to record. He spoke in a form of Mantiran, a beautiful, haunting tongue full of grace and inspiration.

He finally fell silent and slept heavily.

We worked with the record, but it had a star-sound we could not understand. Finally, Harna, an old woman who had once lived in Mantira, came to our living shape and asked to hear it. We played it for her and she began shaking and crying out, and picking at her clothing with her fingers. When the record stopped she said: "It is the Mantirans, the lost Mantirans! The ones that left for the stars! I was there when they were wooed away by the great Roh! How we pleaded with them, crying to them not to leave but to remain and serve Earth. We wanted them to find earth love before leaving, to be fulfilled before going to the cosmos, but they would not listen. They left and have not been heard of since, until now — now they are speaking to us about star energy, which they want more of. Their appetites have grown. They say that if other humans join them they will be able to attract and hold even greater amounts of that energy. So they are coming here to Mebora to enlist some of our young, to carry them away from us. I hear them! They will plunder this land of its young and beautiful!" And she fell at our feet, weeping and exhausted.

Five days later lights were seen in the sky and a shape descended. It landed and four men appeared. They were human, but so different. Draped in star substance and glittering with cosmic jewels, they stood before us and spoke slowly, extolling their way of life in the vast spaces. They said that humans are destined to command those areas, for human energy is tremendously effective there. However, due to overuse their own energy was low, so more humans were needed to bring the activities to a new level of accomplishment. They assured us that the new converts would gain treasure unimaginable and be given magnificent power!

But Drena, our teacher, arose and said, "Tell us, do you experience Azar's love there? Do you commune with Him, and are you one with His other creatures there? Do you act as Azar's sons should, training your young in the loving ways of service? Or do you spend your energy creating power positions and gaining control over areas of substance? Are you commanding or are you helping? Are you controlling or are you allowing?

"And do you ever spend a night with Azar, as we do occasionally, being alone in the warm night with Azar, talking and listening, clearing away any misunderstandings; and in the morning find yourselves refreshed and starting new ventures in partnership with Him? Do you ever do this?

"No, you probably do not, since you are working with the Azar of energy rather than the Azar of love. Not that these are separate Azars. They are not, for He is One. But we are instructed to work with Azar's energy only after we are open to and guided by His love; otherwise we would act blindly and work through the lower finite self, which is faulty and full of error.

"So do not ask us to go with you. Ask rather if you may stay here with us, establishing yourselves first in service and love, then going to the stars as completed men, working for Azar, not for your own smaller selves!"

But the light had shifted in their eyes, and they were wary and closed. A veil of secrecy was over them. They talked persuasively of their ways among the stars, singling out young untried ones for their solicitations. But all stood firm, for Drena was sustaining a level of protective energy around us. They finally departed, returning through the sky. We sent with them our best wishes, for they were our brothers and we wished them well.

PRAYER 2

Azar,

Our ways extend to You. We follow Your Plan in its holy simplicity.

Wanting You above all, we pause and address You hourly, and You answer with touches of love.

A mist of affection clouds our vision and a thrill of belonging fires our being. We are immersed in Your approval.

The sound of Your voice moves us strangely. We constantly walk toward You.

When our breath falters, we wait patiently, knowing that Yours will sustain us.

Your concern embraces us; we are caught in a cloud of care.

Your sweetness at times is blinding, but we travel on into it, trusting Your guidance.

Surely goodness and beauty shall follow us throughout our days, and we will dwell in Your Soul forever.

CHILDREN OF THE NARRAN

We saw the colors again the next day. Translucent balls of color, gathered in the upper branches like nests of birds. They seemed to belong to the sky, to somewhere away from here. In their movements, their flutterings, they were like exotic birds huddled in the air, protected by the strength of the earth trees.

They were from another time frame. By accident they had entered Earth's atmosphere through an opening, a leakage point from their own environment. There are several of these openings connecting us to adjacent frames.

These circular shapes were embryos. They were children of the Narran, who live in the time frame next to Earth, opposite the Zin. The Narran are a floating race, moving through the air, not quite touching down. (Their planet is another dimension of Earth, solid but vibrating at a slightly different rate.) The spiritual states of the Narran are reflected in their buoyancy, their freedom from the ground. The more spiritual they become, the higher they can ascend, moving through the air by spontaneous mind control. The less spiritual they are, the nearer they stay to the ground. Thus their state is observed at a glance and they are treated accordingly. Authorities are chosen according to their spiritual degree, and if they slip (or, should we say, drop) they are immediately removed from office. It is the same with all managers, supervisors, teachers, all persons of responsibility.

The Narran have scanned our life extensively and have been appalled at our inability to perceive our own qualities and attributes. They realize that we have no obvious way of discriminating in the choice of leaders, that we can only fall back upon a rudimentary hunch level, an undependable liking or disliking. They say we are fated to fail, for our mistakes outnumber our successes.

So the translucent shapes huddled under the branches, desolate in their separation from their own environment. Soon it was birthing time, and the shells opened and small beings floated out: tiny, perfectly formed, near-human in appearance. In their new-found freedom they glided and soared through the atmosphere, not knowing that in their own vibration their sweep would be much grander. They traveled across the countryside happy and content, swaying and flowing through the sweet air of Earth, free and at peace.

Then without knowing, they strayed into a hunting area and were forthwith brought down by hunters so filled with the sickness of destroying that they would aim at an angel if they saw one, and the little ones fell to earth, expiring! The hunters, seeing their bodies, were seized with horror and hastily buried them, then fled the area, feeling sick and abased, never looking into each other's eyes again.

So now an aura of guilt hangs over Earth. It cannot dissipate, for men are still performing this same action.

Whenever they take the shine out of the eyes of any children (young or old) by being impatiently or cynically cruel to them, then they are as surely as heaven shooting them down out of the sky, tumbling them from their happinesses, their innocent contentments, letting them fall bruised and wounded to die in the warm air of our lovely, gracious planet Earth.

But they no longer bury them.

THE GOLDEN HOLINESS

When the Golden Holiness comes upon you, you will be amazed and say, "What is this, this rapture inside me that seems to be trying to burst and tear me asunder?"

Then the Mighty One will smile and say, "Your Golden Holiness is Me entering into you, playing within you, exploring your being with love and anticipation, getting familiar with you, knowing the glorious things that we shall be doing together, you and I, for we shall walk in the hitchstep of love, you and I, and we will smile and touch each other, you and I (O my child, my child from the lost woods of desire, from the ravines of despair, from the snowfields of desolation!).

"Now that you are walking freely, I am entering you, claiming my own after a sad time of separation, after a futile period of nonawareness, after your centuries of ego-wishes that have turned to ashes, dust to dust. Now you are ready, ready to be mine and I will be yours, my love, my holy one, and you *are* my holy one for you *do* have my glory within you. My holy happiness *is* within you, and lo, I knock and your door opens outward for me and I enter, and we sup together and exchange memories, my sweet child, and all, all is love and goodness, and the Golden Holiness is come upon you!"

THE NEBUNAR

The once-proud Nebunar came down the hill from Holtar with drums quiet, flags stilled and pennants wrapped, and with expressions of uncertainty. They hurried into the military square and on into the barrack rooms, allowing no ceremony, no pomp. Their eyes were veiled, their glances inward.

We waited for them to emerge — we, their families and friends — but they remained within. We could hear sounds of conversation, even argument at times. Finally, after many hours during which Elysius' wife waited with us, pacing, an orderly came out with a large inked document which he attached to the announcing board. It read:

    "To the citizens of Nebuna. Let this inform you that we, the army of Nebuna, do now establish principles for our thinking and rules for our behavior. We are heeding the desires of Azar, our benefactor, and are

following His ways of love.

"Henceforth this army will be used for defense only, and then only after a long period of conferring, of trying to avoid force by diplomatic means.

"We have found that force is avoidable, that Azar has given us other ways with which to settle disagreements. He has explained to us that differences are simply opportunities for love to be expressed and brotherhood to be established; that we should embrace all disagreements and differences, letting them lead us toward true Being.

"So we hereby declare that force shall be a last resort only. We are setting up a Board of Conference which will review all misunderstandings, allowing antagonists to be heard and respected. This Board will be available to all who need it, and all will be welcomed.

"We dedicate ourselves to settlement rather than to slaughter. We now encase our weapons, and will use them only in direst emergency.

"Fellow citizens, may you recognize the truth of this declaration and abide by it in peace.

"A-mena."

TOBI

And when Tobi was come back to Tanivar, with wide, deep eyes and glorious expression, we wondered at him. His spirit was open and flowing strongly, and as he stepped down from his conveyance he took our hands and spoke gravely.

"O my people, I have been in the land of the Mantira where the mountain speaks with fire, and have seen a vision and felt a rapture that has swelled my heart so that at times I hardly breathe. I am now connected with Azar, directly connected with Azar! Look!"

He pointed above, and we saw a thin trail of white energy emanating from his head, trailing upward into space.

"This is the connection I sought," he said, "when I took myself to the mountain slope and out of great love for Azar stated that I would not leave that place until I had gained intimate knowledge of Him. I sat and meditated, occasionally moving just enough to keep the body functioning, and time passed, days and nights. Through all of this I constantly sent my desire to Azar, to the noble Azar, to honor me and let me at last know Him.

"Finally He did.

"He entered my being, gently at first, like the sun breaking over the land. Then moving confidently, He invaded my every area with authority, and I sat quietly, gratified and full with love for Him. He revealed truths, explained causes and effects, and shared intimacies beyond imagining. He then announced that I was now dedicated to His service and was therefore one of His earth angels, that we were now permanently joined, and ever would be.

"So here I am, in His service, come to tell you of these things, and to suggest that all who so desire follow me to the land of the Mantira and up the mountain there. I will guide you, and bring you to the same experience."

A number of young men declared to go with him, old Eman as well, and the next day they left full of high spirits and glorious hopes. The rest of us looked at each other in silence, then looked away. Later in the quiet of my room the tears came. My heart wept as I realized that I had again failed Azar.

But then a voice spoke, saying, "*Some may go and some must stay. All things must be done, so grieve not. Be at peace.*"

This comforted me; yet my heart has never felt the same, and daily I watch the cleft in the hills for the soldiers of Azar, both desiring and dreading their return.

DID YOU KNOW?

Did you know that arrests have been frequent, that the invaders are tolling the bridges and fastening the gates, that all are being slowly crushed into indifference and marked with pain?

Yes, the way is troublesome in your world, the world of the finite, unknowing earth people. For you are stunted and sometimes base. The invaders are ever sure in their cunning, their elusiveness, their certainty. They doubt not, for they are completely mired in the false.

Do not resist their restrictions; just walk away from them. Join not your mind to theirs. If they do you harm, you will be whole again later and will not have been truly touched by their trampling feet and bruising fingers.

Abstain from them. They are from the center of the earth.

THE FLOWERING

From the Nebunar record:

The Alternate Way is now known. We saw it manifested in one of the valleys of Mora ten turnings ago.

We were on an exploring expedition, working for the Council of Nebuna. The purpose was to see if Mora would serve as an expansion area for our enlarging Nebunar population.

Our numbers have been increasing, thanks to the urgings of the Council of Three. Citizens are given honorariums for each child born, for we Nebunar are determined to become a large nation and an important one, one to be honored and feared by the other nations of this subcontinent.

We have not fared well since our invasion of Holtar. No, after the curious conclusion of that episode our confidence seemed to leave us. We became uncertain. We would go to the temples and ask to be given back our former assurance, but all the priests would say was, "Ask Azar. Approach Him as a humble son or daughter. Ask Him to lead you toward joy and love, toward oneness with Him."

This, however, was not what we wanted. We needed, rather, to feel important again, to once more feel that we mattered in this part of the world. Our poise had been shaken by the ignominious conclusion of the invasion. Elysius, our military leader at that time, soon retired from his position and began teaching in an obscure temple in the south. Teaching love and justice, of all things!

Our Council finally pulled itself together and elected Harnan, a no-nonsense person, as leader. Harnan immediately began working to restore Nebunar prestige. He started by confiscating all copies of the notorious declaration written by Elysius and his men at the conclusion of the invasion. (They are now destroyed and no more may be printed.) He then vowed to rebuild the Nebunar "mystique." No one knew exactly what this meant, but it included touring troupes of Nebunar dancers, gymnasium programs to glorify the bodies of our youth, and, of course, incessant encouragement of a larger population.

So since there will soon be a need for more land for our people, we were sent to explore the mountains and valleys of Mora to see if they would serve the Nebunar purposes.

We set out in a determined manner. Nothing much happened the first few days; the topography was monotonous, the vegetation dull. However, on the fifth day something unusual did occur. We stumbled by chance upon a valley of curious atmosphere, a place serenely strange, yet hauntingly familiar.

Its discovery came about in an unusual way. Serna, turning to reach a tree fruit, happened to glimpse a faint path disappearing into the cliff. Following it, she passed through a hidden cleft in the rock and entered a passageway that led through and into a valley, a spacious, beautiful valley. She called to us and we followed.

Feeling strangely peaceful and happy, we dropped our packs in order to better enjoy this lovely place, for it was a paradise! Trees were bearing fruit, and ground growths were heavy with harvest. Streams ran through the valley, spreading water everywhere. Animals, gentle and loving, came up to us with bright-eyed confidence, seeking our caress. Menor wanted to kill one for our next nourishment, but we said: "Why bother, when sustenance is here to be picked from the trees and bushes or pulled from the ground? And would you look at the size of these turins?"

The ground foods were amazing. And their flavor! We decided to take some of their seed back to Nebuna.

Wandering through the valley, we looked, tasted, and exclaimed. Then Serna noticed smoke ahead, a thin stream rising into the sky. Menor was sent back for our weapons, which we had somehow left on the trail behind us. As soon as he returned with them we moved forward cautiously, alert for any trouble. The trail widened, then opened into a large clearing, and there in front of a dwelling stood a man, a woman, and a girl calmly observing us.

We circled them to get a tactical advantage, but they simply smiled and greeted us in our own tongue. They were from Nebuna! We were so happy to find our own here: Advance pioneers for the great state of Nebuna! But when we greeted them thusly, the man said: "No, we do not belong to Nebuna, we belong to Azar and therefore are members of all countries, all races, all humankind. Azar is our Father and all men are our brothers. The entire world is our home."

"But you are Nebunar!" we exclaimed.

"We are Azarians first and Nebunar or Holtar or whatever, second."

"Azarians?"

"Yes, Azarians! Is this so hard to understand?" He

smiled warmly. "We belong to Azar the Magnificent. We have served Him on Earth many times, in many places. He is our leader, our Shining One!"

"Well, all of we Nebunar believe in Azar. He is our God also!"

"No," the man said, "He is not your God. You are, rather, His people. You belong to Him, not Him to you. All starts with Azar. He existed first, then created us, His children, His family, His companions. All Earth is Azar's country. There is no separate Nebuna, Mantira, or whatever. There is only the Land of Azar and its inhabitants, the Azarians. So welcome to another part of His land! Our love to you." They moved impulsively to embrace us, but we stepped aside, keeping our weapons ready.

Laughing good-naturedly at our reactions, they went to the cooking fire and began serving up food with an indescribably delicious odor — and taste, when we finally summoned the nerve to try it. It tasted like...well, it is difficult to describe. Is it possible for food to taste like feelings? Is it? For this food did. It tasted the way wonderful feelings feel. Like the way one feels upon graduating from training school, or the way one's heart sings at dawn after a night of love, or the way one's child looks when seeing the moon for the first time. It tasted clean, joyous, and — and wonderful! This is all I can say.

The woman said, "This food has been provided by Azar; it is from Him to you. One of His helpers, who is our guide at present, told us how to prepare it. We will share this information with you if you wish. However, it probably can be used only with this valley's produce, which is truly blessed by Azar.

"Now, do not be confused. We all know that the entire world, in fact the entire cosmos, is blessed by Azar! However, I am speaking of a very special blessing. You see, some time ago we gave ourselves over to Him entirely. With no reservations we allowed Him to make of us what He willed, to bring us to flower, so to speak. Which He did. He brought us into His Being, into His glory! Alleluia!" And her eyes glowed and sang.

"Since then He has turned over to us a certain degree of influence over the creatures and growing things here in this valley. He lets their flowering come as a response to our flowering, and their confidence as a result of our trust. The fruits and vegetables you are enjoying have moved to their own true state, inspired by our acceptance of perfection. They are joyous, and sing with us a song of praise to Azar!

"You see, it is finished here, all is accomplished here. This valley is in full flower. According to our guides it is the only place on Earth that has truly opened all the way to Azar. The All of Him is not rebuffed here as it is in your land. (For some reason earth people feel they have the right to refuse Azar!)

"Yes, Azar is completely accepted here, if it may be said in this manner, and He is, in turn, completely open to us. And you, because you are here, will now start to open and accept, for within you is the same desire for perfection. Your finite beliefs cannot resist the truth that is manifesting here."

"But we could invade this valley, we of the Nebunar!" we exclaimed.

"No, you could not," the man said. "Don't you see that your foolish desire for acquisition could not in any way affect this place? Once Azar has brought a part of Earth to a complete flowering, then its perfection is invincible and cannot be touched by the limited ways of man. Certainly not by your people — witness your abortive invasion of the Holtar, who turned you back without weaponry simply by using unconditional love. If you cannot invade their land, which is still in transition to Azar, then how could you invade this valley, which is competely open to Him?

"Actually, you were allowed to find this valley, for you are ready for our teachings. All of you have had many livings here on Earth and have risen to a point near the level of awakening. All you need do now is discard your present blind allegiance to temporal authority. Simply abandon it, transferring its dedication and service to Azar. This you can and shall do.

"Many changes will then come about in your natures, many new ways of being will occur. For instance, at this time you cannot see the adjacent planes with their guides and helpers; in the future you will be able to do so. You will then realize that this area is not just a section of Earth to be seized by small earth humans and done with as they please. No, this area has been opened, and therefore belongs to all the beings and planes that connect with it, that impinge upon it. They would not allow its high condition of perfection to be marred by the grasping hands of a few earth grubs!

"Realize that you were brought here as a step toward the fulfillment of a great Plan. A Plan to expand the qualities of this valley outward, so that they may begin to encompass other areas of Earth. You are the beginning of the new ones to be trained toward perfection. We salute you, you favored ones of Azar."

He made a strange gesture with his hands, almost like a benediction, and the air grew misty and began to glow. A bell sound filled our ears, and we saw many beings around us, on the earth and in the sky. They seemed to be welcoming us somehow, to be acknowledging us in some way, and we felt a love for them as well as a shyness. An ecstasy grew within us, a great, great ecstasy, and we were truly fulfilled!

Later our vision shifted and we were again seeing the valley itself, but oh, how it had changed! Its colors were richer, its beauty more entrancing; it was glorious! We ran this way and that, exclaiming over its marvels. The girl went with us, telling us that this was how Earth had looked to the first man, Adon, many ages ago. However, the small vision of man had since robbed Earth of much of its beauty, at least to his own eyes, and his seeing had gradually through time become dulled and colorless. However, there is now this Open Place, from which full love and beauty can spread, bringing back to the planet its original glory. And even more, for during the past ages Earth's potential has developed and expanded and its flowering will now be as an adult planet, radiant and bountiful!

We walked and wondered in this paradise. The animals played with us, running ahead, then dashing back, the small ones scampering up our bodies as though we were trees, caressing us, rubbing their noses fondly against our faces.

We finally sank down into soft ferns in a clearing and slept, dreaming of the cosmos, of stars upon stars, systems upon systems, all filled with loving beings of every kind that were saying, "Welcome brothers, welcome!" And over all, riding in a cloud of glory, surrounded by a radiance beyond knowing and projecting a love beyond belief, the Divine Face of Azar shone down upon us, bathing us in His own magnificent love!

And so we found the Alternate Way, an alternative to our lives of smallness and sorrow. The only Way, His Way, and we are now within It forever.

The expansion of this openness will grow slowly, through many ages. Gradually its perfection will reach out and encompass all. This place will remain hidden, while teachers and prophesiers go out into the imperfect places, preparing the many earth children for exaltation.

Then finally, one day, Earth will again be His, Azar's, and all will be open, all will be serving, all will be ecstatic, singing in brotherhood with the firmament.

"Alleluia! Alleluia! All praise to our beloved, our total Being, our Azar!"

WHEN THE LAND IS CLEARED

When the land is cleared and omniconsciousness established, there will be dancing in the solar plexus, singing in the chest and shoulders, and an electric humming across the reaches of the mind. All doubt will be released; there will be rejoicing and closer walks.

When the land is cleared and deep, deep slumber is come, the visitors will knock and enter with compassionate respect and admiration. They will close the portals gently, fearing that the breeze of today might scatter the writings of tomorrow.

When the land is cleared Elahat will talk within the hollow; and never again need the daughters climb the gladed rims of other planets, never again need the children move and sigh in cluttered holygrams, and never again will artifices seize the breath and tear the lining of the heart.

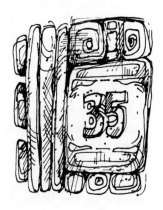

THE ROH FOLLOWERS

The sun was setting as we slipped into the space vault. It was necessary to see the records of the Roh Followers in order to learn of their activities among the stars. They were recruiting again, and we were uneasy at the prospect of yet another contingent of young ones departing into so unknown a future.

The Roh Followers had been allowed a small outpost here in Mantira. Within its area they had constructed a vault for the protection of their equipment and for storing the records of their accomplishments in this part of the universe. We were determined to see these records, so using a little-remembered search law we moved quickly, wanting to be finished before they returned from their current foray in the sky.

The vault was large and well-planned. There were curious objects on the walls and ceilings, obviously artifacts from other planets. We were excited and somewhat apprehensive, for we found this firsthand contact with outer space unnerving. Moving on into the record room, we looked inside the orderly containers and found a rendering of history, the history of their transactions in adjacent cosmic areas. As we read, our eyes clouded with disbelief, then with disgust, and then with sorrow. Slavery in the outer worlds! Man had transported slavery into the cosmos!

There were detailed accounts of the subjugation of various alien peoples in a nearby area of the galaxy and the forcing of them to work for the Followers under threat of destruction. The most appalling case was that of the Zerzans (the records were quite explicit). They were strange creatures with multiple arms and legs who were adept at construction and mining. The Roh Followers, using knowledge of explosive substances (the Porgas), were causing them to mine areas of certain planets and to construct complex shapes for the budding Roh star government. The punishment of a Zerzan rebel was to drop an explosive on his city area, causing the death of his family and friends.

Equally appalling was the fact that the Followers were doing this in the name of Azar. Their argument was that Azar desired the advancement of those areas, that they were simply following His wishes by organizing the haphazard societies of the star people into systematic governments, with the Followers, of course, as rulers and guardians of the star wealth.

The records were written in a pretentious, quasi-religious language that sickened us with its pomp and righteousness. Azar was portrayed as a cold, hard ruler who demanded obedience from the space peoples, and the Roh Followers were presented as His lieutenants who passed His commands down to the awkward and ignorant aliens. There was no warmth or love within these records. All was cold, vengeful, and insistent upon hard work.

So now we knew. They were enslaving people in the

skies, in direct violation of the edicts of Azar. Manipulating poor star creatures that had never known earth evil. Exploiting exotic ones in faraway places, suppressing them into colorless obedience.

We knew we must stop this activity, if possible. If not, then we must remove all connection with it from Earth, for Azar is not to be mocked by His children. So we waited until all of the garrison were back in the city and then, not without struggle, arrested and detained them in our holding rooms. We talked with them for several days, trying to alter their viewpoints, but their eyes were star-struck and their minds covetous. The beauty of our relationship with Azar escaped them.

Finally we told them to return to their accomplices in the stars, that henceforth all Followers were banished from here. We would no longer even recognize them as earthmen, but would instead consider them a form of alien issue not to be allowed in our land at any time. Word of this would be spread everywhere — even, if possible, out among the stars. The actions of the Followers would be known far and wide. They would be abhorrent to all people.

This, however, bothered them not. Their eyes remained hard and defiant as they departed into the skies. We then dismantled, for all time, their space vault.

And so, somewhere among the stars is a group of earthlings exiled from Earth, warm, loving Earth. Their hearts must be quite cold by now, and their handclasps perfunctory. Azar will bring them again to us when their minds and feelings change. Until then we stand adamant, rejecting their presence and denying their ways, for we cannot allow the negatives of this planet to be spread among the other systems.

We have long been fighting the lesser ways of Earth — its destructiveness and its denial of Azar. We must not permit these to spread to purer areas; rather, we must quarantine our blight, for the outer worlds may be deep in their trust of Azar and operating beautifully within His love. If we permit our lesser ways to go among them we will be setting tragedy loose in their worlds, for innocence is a fragile thing that needs protecting.

Until man can obey his basic morality he should be kept to himself and regularly sent teachers. According to our seers, man is unique in his destructiveness and his disregard of the Creator. Let us isolate him until these illnesses are cured. Then we can commence relations with other areas of the universe. Until that time, we will protect the innocents out there from our ways. They do not deserve us as we are now.

As for the Roh Followers at present among the stars, we can only trust that Azar will bring them to their senses before too much damage is done. Perhaps we earthlings needed to see how little we are ready for the stars and how little the stars are ready for us.

One day man will succeed in making of this world a sane, orderly place, allowing it to flower and become the paradise it is intended to be. Once it is stabilized, all calamity and hardship will disappear, for Earth is a self-contained, fully equipped ship of Azar, sailing through His skies, carrying its souls onward to higher realms, to greater glory, to sweeter Oneness with Him.

THE FRIEND

The experience is near, it is coming, coming. We will soon be given the white darkness to receive in. Ever breathing the planet's musings, we will be serene, and give control over to the Friend.

The Friend will respect and cherish us, and we will respect and cherish the Friend. He will care for our private ways, and we will honor his wantings. A love will grow between us, a love of the good, of the giving, of the serving.

We will be ever full of his knowings and helpings, and he will be ever full of our blessings. He will have our loaning, and we will have his using. Let us give praise and honor to — the Friend.

THE EXPANSION OF THE OPENNESS

The way was new and untraveled. We were to sail around the shore to a silver inlet, disembark, and walk exactly five kiloms up the canyon to a high place, arriving there before the moon reached its height.

Precautions were necessary, for the Nebunar Council of Three was watching everything and everybody. Its members, highly suspicious, were probing into all activities in the more remote areas in and near Nebuna. They knew that many did not approve of their policies. The making of Nebuna into a military state was repugnant to many people, who were beginning to withdraw into settlements in the Nebunar hills and in the neighboring Moran valleys.

There was even talk of an unusual kind of settlement in one of the valleys — a settlement open to Azar in some special way. However, no one knew for sure.

We were Mantirans, invited in the name of Azar to meet with one of these groups in a hidden place on the Nebunar border. Being Mantirans, we were dedicated, of course, to the rule of Azar, not of man, and any request in His name was to be honored.

We followed the path up the canyon, ten of us, each aware of the beauty of Azar's land. "It is our land, too," we thought, "for we are a part of Azar."

The moon was serene and lovely, and as we walked we discussed the latest prediction of our seers. They said that at some time in the not-too-distant future, Azar would be sending a most unusual teacher to humanity, perhaps to this very area, if it hadn't been changed too much by planetary conditions. A world teacher, one of His highly placed helpers, would come and inhabit an earth body and teach poor man the ways of love. He would be one of the special sons; it was even thought he might be the legendary First Son of Azar, who has briefly visited Earth and helped humanity in the past.

Thinking these thoughts, we arrived at the meeting place. There was only a young girl there sitting on a slight promontory in a moonlit clearing. She greeted us and asked us to be seated. She then began to glow with beautiful colors, and suddenly seemed to be someone else, an older woman, who spoke in measured tones, with graceful gestures.

"Greetings, brothers and sisters of Earth. I am Listra, from the Higher Realm. I ocasionally use the being of this dear earth child, with her loving permission, in order to communicate directly with this planet. Her bodily vibrations will allow me thirty marens of time to tell you of what is now coming.

"Be aware that at last the flowering of Earth has begun. Yes, there is now an opened area in a nearby Moran valley, where Azar's ways are in full flower. It has taken long ages to prepare this outpost, to cleanse a location where His breath could be free. The universal hosts are chanting in wonder. From this Open Place are to go forth teachers and prophets to the far reaches of Earth, who will start preparing the rest of the planet for openness. This will take several ages, during which there will be great upheavals here: physical as well as psychic and mental. However, the opened area will not be touched by that turmoil. Indeed it cannot be, for it is opened and love resides there without hindrance.

"You Mantirans, with your advanced awareness of Azar, will be prominent among these teachers and prophets. Your efforts will establish Near Open locations deep within the various territories of the Lower One, the adversary who fell to Earth some ages ago. He will resist you, but will not essentially touch you, for you will have been in the Open Place and been given of its purest vibrations.

"You will establish centers of truth in many far places. Using the terms appropriate to their languages, you will tell the people in those places about Azar and His Plan. You will draw them along the path and start them moving in the direction of freedom and openness. Those of you who do not have a hearing of the helpers will be given it, for guidance from the Higher Realm is absolutely necessary during this work. You will listen to and obey His angels. It is that simple. There will be some sorrow and suffering, for you will be opposed by powerful forces; however, you will know glory unbelievable, and the very highest sensitivity. Your names will be sung in Heaven.

"First, though, you will go the Open Place to be perfected, and will remain there to receive the bliss of Azar. You then will disperse to your assigned places to start this movement toward Azar, several of you going into the primary city of Nebuna where the Council of Three is fast approaching insanity. With your acquired followers you will serve as an anchor point during the coming tribulation.

"Dear ones, it is my privilege to serve Azar upon this

planet, and to have contact with the beautiful earth people, beautiful, though marred by darkness.

"Now I must go. Farewell, and my love to you!"

Her transposed features faded, and the face of the young girl was again prominent. She smiled shyly and held out her hands to us, saying, "Come, let us join the others." She then led us through the trees to a house in the rocks, a humble house where a small group greeted us warmly and gave us food, drink, and resting places.

We talked excitedly of our new destination, the Open Place. They assured us the experience would be final, for we at last would be in touch with Perfection, the gleaming goal of all human beings.

We knew that in the work following we would need great strength and resolve, for the way would be long and heavy with difficulties. However, we would be serving the Ultimate, the very Ultimate and for the first time in our lives would be walking completely in the sun, with no shadows to hide our paths.

And the return would be almost overwhelming. We would know the bliss of the Presence, and we would be in direct contact with those of the Higher Realm, probably both hearing and seeing them.

"So, Father, point us the way and tell us the starting time, for we are ready for Your Will. May we ever heed and follow you, ever praise and honor you, until the end without end of this endless world.

"Forever and ever, A-mena, Amen."

PRAYER 3

Dear Azar,

May I know the measure of Your love.

May I know the ways You reach me,
the ways You touch me,
the ways You teach me.

In my house of glass
I rise to greet You,
in light so bright I walk to meet You.

You are my chalice, I am Your dove.

AZON

The ways of the Pardu glitter. Their forms are winsome, their speech liquid; they glow at night. Yes, when sunlight leaves they radiate slightly. This is a result of the Porgas wars in which they were passive and helpful to both sides and so were not fired upon, but yet received large amounts of drifting radiation.

Their harbors are clean, their ships sturdy. Their temples are largely unused, as they feel no great need for Azar. However, some day they will falter, and need will come. Then He will open Himself to them. Until that time they will function well and continue to perpetuate themselves.

On a particular day we were walking in the hills of Pardu looking for ancient shrines. This was in an area once active in the worship of Azon, the Sun, and remnants of sun symbols could sometimes be found in the ruins of the shrines. We wandered into a valley we had never noticed before. It was long and narrow, and as we progressed we became uneasy, not liking cliffs so close above us. After awhile it opened out, and ahead of us were three elevations with leveled tops. We found a path going up the third one and climbed, wondering. Reaching the top, we moved toward the center and came to a wide place, a gentle place where the light was soft and constant. Nothing moved there, neither air, creature, nor growing thing. All was still with a warm stillness, a readiness. We stood in the center and waited, scarcely breathing, and it began.

Drums and flutes sounded and we could see dim shapes moving — circles of phantom men, weaving and intermingling — and the light from the Sun became bright and resistless, penetrating our very thoughts. It seemed to say to us, "I am your sign, your beacon. Give to me your selves and I will fill them. Receive me in my giving and you will be as I am, as Azon is!"

The light pushed at us, and we joined the circles of the shadow figures. They became more real and we saw that they were men of glowing energy, with wide eyes and sweet smiles. They dressed in loose tunics and moved ecstatically. We loosened our clothing so that the Sun could be nearer, and feeling an indescribable longing, opened our hearts, asking the great Azon to come into us. We moved with the rest, our lines like serpentine flowings circling and crossing. Finally we all stopped and put our clothing aside. Standing motionless, we were in fullest intimacy with Him, and He enveloped us in a blinding gust of ecstatic energy-love. Our bodies responded in the fullest way they could, and we were transfigured! We were gods, a part of the great Sun, the blinding, loving, terrible Sun!

We remained transfixed, our eyes like stars turning to all the corners of the sky and to each other in wonderment. Then the unearthly ecstasy began to subside. We raised our arms and clasped them together in an unusual manner, and saw our shadow companions doing the same. Suddenly the entire world seemed to be raising and clasping its arms to Azon and His bright streams of golden energy flowed down and around, filling the air with glorious radiance and holy love.

Finally our arms dropped, the energy lessened, and we were alone, the shadow figures having slipped away.

Returning to ourselves, we sat for a long time in the twilight calm of this place, this holy place of the past, a place to be seldom seen, for the past is not the now. Yet curiously we knew that this past had somehow fulfilled our now, and that perhaps it was proper to occasionally reenter the past as we just had. And we knew that in the future others, led by inner needs, would find their way here and also reenact the ancient ceremony. They too would be joined by the shadow men whose images, fired by the intense ceremonial energy of the past, still exist and wait here, waiting to be raised by living worshippers, the worshippers of Azon the Great, the Bountiful, the Light of all Lights!

Occasionally, in an old worship place such as this, new ones call forth His intimate ray. Then He reenacts His ancient ceremony, creating a oneness, a personal love relationship with some of the growing children of Earth whose needs He can so fulfill at times.

And the totality of Azar smiles and watches the wonder and ecstasy of these small ones on the middle planet, and continues His brooding over the All with assurance and peace.

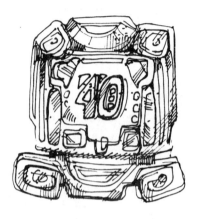

When the time is done and the changes made you will be as fire on the mountain, as water rolling across the land.

There will be no one you are stranger to, no one you are not lover to, no one not a part of you.

Force will no longer threaten you, fear no longer hinder you, and Light no longer blind you.

You will be ecstatic and amazed.

You will see the all, the everything, and Love will fall upon you.

Never wanting, never doubting, never too surely knowing, you will be ever safe and strong.

THE COMING CHANGES

When Zara fell through the sky, we trembled and breathed shallowly. We breathed shallowly, slowing the flow of the red wine of life. This moved us to a position on the diagonal, which would open us to portents.

They came, the messages, winging from the Higher Realm. We stood absolutely still, acting as grateful receiving centers. The connections were made, and the thoughts began flowing into our beings. We received differently, individually. Later we matched the pieces together.

We were told that Earth was now to undergo a cyclical cleansing in preparation for a future age; that there would be upheavals of land and water, creating new shapes and configurations and causing our way of living to change drastically.

We were to prepare writings of our science and mystery knowledge as well as of our knowings of the spirit, and implant them in the earth under a gigantic triangular shape that we, with Their help, would raise. This would be a finely calibrated marker, a signal to the future. The upheavals would not destroy it but would flow around it, and some day in the far future these writings would be uncovered by a world thirsting for true knowledge.

We were informed that our race would need to become a nomadic hunter race through a long period, existing with confidence on little. And that we would lose to a great extent our special knowledge, this being necessary and inevitable. However, the warm and shining quality of our life would be preserved in the Higher Realm, then one day brought from its matrix there to again manifest on Earth. This would occur only after the Master Teacher had appeared and prepared mankind for the higher ways.

We were told that most of us would at that time serve as guides from the Other Place and the Higher Realm, helping the people of Earth to again manifest the ways of Azar. There then would be a culmination, and the very soil of Earth would begin to transmute, moving at a finer vibratory rate which would be a setting for incarnations of a higher level, incarnations of beings from another system who would need Earth's special medicinal properties. (The herbal qualities of Earth are unique in the universe, matched only by the planet Darius in the westerly sector, using Neptune as the point of north.)

So we bound our heads and dedicated ourselves to our future, a future of preparation and change and of opportunity for ever fuller service to our Total Being, our Azar.

AND NOW THAT WE ARE GONE

And now that we are gone from there, from Earth, our remembering is not of the things we were so often aware of: the pain, the fear, the sorrow. No, it is of the love in people's eyes, the warmth of people's handclasps, the joy of people laughing, and the tenderness of family love with all the members gathered together. We know that Azar's Love is there, shining in men's souls and lighting their somber days and worried nights.

So for all of Earth we smile and turn our hearts toward that lovely planet with its strange hopes, its homeless ways, its lonely spirits waiting for the All.

We salute you, our Mother. May you ever G L O W !

EPILOGUE: LATER

The highway crossed many hills, a ribbon of concrete snaking through winding ways and rushing over high places. Cars traveled it at furious speeds, synchronized with terrible efficiency. If one fell out of line due to mechanical failure, its occupants would wait until a repair vehicle appeared, and would soon be moving again, feeling assured and successful.

The driver of one such machine, a doctor named Maronn, stalled on a high incline, became impatient and decided to walk about a bit. He gazed at the beautiful scenery and, seeing a stream below, descended. As he reached the stream he heard movement. Looking around he saw someone nearby, a young man dressed simply, with an air of strange intensity about him. The young man looked at him alertly, nodded in greeting, then stepped into the trees and was gone.

The doctor called out, but there was no answer. Curious, he moved in that direction and walked down a path that suddenly appeared, a path that led off into the distance, winding around clefts and ravines and through lush meadows. He was entranced by the terrain, having never seen any quite like it before. He also felt calmed by an unusual peace and serenity in the air.

Determined to see where the path led, he kept walking. After awhile he came to an elevated area, which he climbed with some difficulty. Reaching the top he saw before him a shallow valley, a quiet wooded area, with buildings clustered among the trees — houses, apparently, but strange in shape and decoration. He walked down among them in wonderment, and the people there looked at him in the same way. They wore peculiar clothing, and called to him in strange tones and inflections. He could not understand them, nor they him, and he began to feel a bit uneasy. Then the young man reappeared.

He spoke slowly in the doctor's tongue, smiling gently. He told him that this was a settlement ages old, that its people had been here for untold centuries and had never been in open contact with Maronn's people — the machine people, as they called them. The construction of the highway had brought the machine people closer, but privacy here had been maintained due to the trees and winding hills. He told Maronn he was the first of the machine people ever to approach the settlement and that he was welcome if he would promise not to tell of them later.

The doctor agreed, being a thoughtful person. He asked why they had not joined his world instead of living here like primitives. The young man laughed and said, "Primitives? These people are much more sophisticated than you machine people! They have developed *themselves*, while your people have developed mechanisms. They can do most of what your machines do using just their hands, minds, and spirits. Come, let me show you."

The young man, Zerin, led him through the settlement and showed him the many exotic buildings, with strange and unusual walkways between. Maronn was amazed at a most involved system of hanging fruit and vegetable gardens and at various odd contrivances apparently used in the making of clothing and the preparation of food. It was a civilization quite unlike his own, fascinating in its color, vitality, and simplicity.

He asked about medical facilities and was led to a round building with a plant signet on its door. Zerin remarked that the building was the equivalent of a hospital, with the signet that of a healing plant. Suggesting they observe a healing that was about to occur, he opened the door and they entered, joining a small group of people waiting there. Soon a woman was brought in. One of her legs was malformed, causing a grotesque limp. Zerin explained that she lived further down the river and that her people had only recently been coming to the Manteer, as this group was called, for help. He said she was to be healed by spiritual means "unlike your ways, with your anesthetics, cutting knives, bone grafts, and plastic insertions."

The others, twelve in number, gathered in a circle around the woman. Speech, an apparent talking to the invisible, was followed by a period of quiet, in which a curious atmosphere gathered. After awhile the leader touched the woman, and the air came alive with energy. He rotated the leg while another held her hip stationary. The leg was now pliable and moved easily into a normal position. Maronn was told to touch it. He found the flesh quite warm and vibrating strongly. They held the leg in the corrected position for a period of time; when released it remained there.

"She will rest for awhile; then you will see the results of the healing," Zerin said. "Now let us have some refreshment."

They went to another building where people were seated at long tables, eating. Joining them, they had their meal and talked. Maronn asked about the heat in the woman's leg and Zerin answered, "That was the healing energy."

"Where does it come from?"

"It comes from the upper places, the invisible planes. Sometimes we can see into them with our inner eyes, and what we see is indescribably glorious. Actually, the plane nearest us is where we go to when we leave here. The beings there are interested in us, and help us by sending higher, purer energies when we are doing our healings. They, in effect, borrow them from higher up, ultimately from God, then filter them down to us here after converting them into a vibrational rate we can use. This furnishes us with the unbelievable power you saw in action, a power which, when applied to a distorted body, changes its state to that of the imprint of normalcy that overlays it. This imprint is upon every physical body, no matter how far away from it the body has moved. The heat is the vibrational rate of the flesh being increased by the higher frequencies. Not only is the patient affected by these frequencies, but also the other persons participating, for the healing vibrations pass through them as well."

By evening the woman was walking normally, though hesitantly. She seemed overcome by the experience, her eyes clouding with gratitude. Dr. Maronn examined her and was amazed at her recovery. He then told Zerin that he himself was suffering from a malignancy, and had been driving to another city to inquire into a possible new treatment when his machine had failed.

"That can be fixed quite easily," said Zerin. "The healing group is meeting again this evening to treat a person with impaired vision. Two can be healed as easily as one. Come."

And so Maronn lay on one of the couches in the healing room, within the circle of twelve. The leader touched him, and he felt an inner thrill as a current passed through him. Then a tremendous calm was within, as though a wrongness deeply centered in his body had been righted. At that instant he knew the malignancy was gone.

Later they talked, and Zerin said, "We do nothing. We simply ask for help from the universe and then accept it. You see, the other planes and places are filled with beings who receive great joy from helping others. It is only on Earth and a few other hidden-away places that helping is complicated and is held to be of questionable value. The reason for this is that earth living fosters the illusion of separateness. It brings about a sense of separate ego, which makes it difficult to ask for and receive help or even to give help. For these actions — asking, receiving, giving — are essentially non-ego actions and therefore difficult within Earth's vibration. For their basic nature is selfless as opposed to the earth people's fantasy of separate selfhood, with its tendency to believe that accepting help or even giving help is an indication of inner weakness.

"Let us realize that help is a very personal thing. Dealing with it starts one on a path leading away from this separateness. You see, in the process of helping others we give them a bit of ourselves, and in return receive a bit of them back through their gratitude. By the same token, when we are helped we receive a part of the helper, and we send back, through our gratitude, a part of ourselves. In other words, some of the giver wings along with the gift, and some of the receiver sails back to the giver. These interchanges become permanent in the persons involved. They ultimately bring about the feeling of oneness among people — for when bits and pieces of oneself are scattered about among many others and their bits and pieces are in us, then one day it suddenly becomes clear that we all are simply one being, one person.

"Now, these interchanges can occur only when the giver and the receiver are at least partially open to each other. Usually they are. However, upon occasion one or the other will block this personal interchange through fear or arrogance, and then negative results can occur. If a giver refuses to feel the warmth of giving and to accept the returning gratitude, or if a receiver refuses to be grateful and thus acknowledge the giver, then disharmony arises. This refusal to allow the completion of a spiritual action develops in time a canker in the very soul of the person refusing.

"This is the reason for the rule that the giver must never be pressed into giving but must give spontaneously, and then only when asked (either by word, gesture, look, or thought) and that the receiver must never be pushed into accepting but must spontaneously reach out for and then gratefully accept that help. These safeguards ensure that both persons will be at least somewhat open at the time of the action, which then allows the further interchange to take place.

"Those of us who know these truths try to enlighten others, as do those on the other planes. The result is that bit by bit mankind is being brought around and pointed in this true direction, the direction of giving and receiving, of sanity and health.

"And now let us find a place for you to rest."

Dr. Maronn stayed with the Manteer for several weeks. The men moved his machine away from the highway to prevent its attracting notice and causing a search. He was welcomed throughout the settlement. Observing the people, he felt stirrings of regret at his own inner barrenness. Why couldn't he have the same sweet trust and confidence, the same shining faith? The answer was that he knew what would have to give way in his life in order to acquire these qualities, and his worldly side shuddered at the thought of giving up the pleasures that his position, with its prerogatives of money, prestige, and influence, made available to him. He had one of the finest homes in the city, which he enjoyed exploiting in his quest for the the hedonistic satisfactions available within his culture's brittle society.

Zerin was amused. "You want to retain the way of life that brought you the malignancy? In that case the illness probably will recur, and then what will you do? Perhaps you won't be able to find your way back here, or if you do the Others may not choose to be used again as a temporary help. You see, whenever one indulges in selfish apartness from the Source, one draws negativity close and sooner or later suffers some sort of malfunction. It so happens that cell balance is a weak spot in your system; therefore the negative force settled there. With others it could be one of many things. It could manifest as a viral disease, a mental aberration, or possibly an accident of some kind. Didn't your political leader recently hurt himself while boating? Well, that has the same root cause as your malignancy — trying to live a separate existence, with no true involvement with others or with God."

The doctor listened but was not convinced. He returned to his own world, the world of machinery, of hurry and falsity, of shoving, pushing greed. He waxed fat and content and gained a reputation as a host, an arranger of highly sophisticated social events.

After several years the sickness returned, bringing with it shock, despair, and a feeling of shame at his foolishness in not heeding the words of Zerin. He stopped everything and withdrew into solitude, spending long hours meditating. He finally came to a decision. He *would* follow the ways of the Manteer. He would completely turn himself over to the universe, putting his trust in God, doing what *He* wished, and allowing Him to decide whether or not he would be healed again.

He then walked out into the world, letting his feet follow the Source's bidding and take him wherever they willed. They took him down strange streets and into little known byways, where he was amazed to see people hungry and ill from poverty. He had never been aware that such conditions existed in his city. Something told him to help, and his heart moved in answer. He now knew what he was to do.

Renting a dilapidated building, he brought in medicines and food supplies, giving of them freely to those in want. He sold his practice and possessions and moved to this impoverished area, living among his poor, hopeless charges, giving encouragement to tired minds and healing to sick bodies. Time went by, and he bothered not about his health, for he had turned it over to God. He was neither happy nor unhappy, he was simply — fulfilled.

One day as he was busy with his people, he looked up and saw Zerin standing and watching him with radiant eyes and glowing face.

"So, you have done it! You have done it after all!!"

"Done what?" he asked blankly.

"Given yourself over to the universe," cried Zerin, seizing him and holding him closely. "You are one of us now!"

"One of you?" the doctor said in amazement, "Why, what do you mean?"

"You are now one of the children that care for the other children! One of the Father's helpers helping those needing help."

"But I am only doing what I want to do," he said.

"Yes, and the Father is very pleased. Look! Can you not see?" Zerin gestured up and around in a circle. "He is smiling down on you, loving you sweetly and deeply. Yes, the Source is smiling at you and touching you, inspiring you, being you. You are now Him and He is You!"

And suddenly Maronn did see. He saw that he was in the Being of Azar, the Source, and that Azar *was* smiling, and that His smile was in everything — in the radiance of the sun, the shine of the earth, and the beauty of human faces, even those ill and unhappy. Yes, everything was smiling; the trees were smiling, the far-off mountains were smiling, even the crowded tenement buildings were smiling!

And he was finally, finally home.

And so in another instance the awareness of Oneness appeared in this world of separateness, of isolation. Its appearance now occurs more easily, since the teachings of the last great Teacher are still current. Also, some of the ancient techniques are active, being used once more in the search for truth.

The primary awareness being brought forth is that regardless of wars, of pestilences, of man-made barrennesses, the universe is a place of warmth and love, a place where a myriad of beings, visible and invisible, are working together, helping each other, supporting one another, becoming one in harmony and love.

And the All is here brooding over us, leaning into our thoughts, edging into our feelings, working with us, in us, as us. We wait for It to unfold Its ways, to show Its colors, to present Its beauties. Its warmth moves in upon us, and our various judgings and condemnings cease. They step aside and listen as a quiet radiance within us speaks of peace — and there is peace, profound and prepared, a peace that has been waiting since the beginning that never was. Waiting for beings to live in it, to be it.

And so we are at last truly alive and truly ready for the universe. Our universe, which always has been and ever shall be — G O D.